PRAISE FOR LUKE MARSH

From *"100+ Unexplained Mysteries for Curious Minds:"*

Luke Marsh's "100+ Unexplained Mysteries for Curious Minds" is an enthralling and informative journey through the most captivating enigmas of our world. It is a must-read for anyone with a thirst for knowledge and a fascination with the unexplained. Whether you're a skeptic seeking to challenge your beliefs or a believer seeking validation, this book offers an irresistible invitation to explore the uncharted territories of the mind. Delve into its pages, and prepare to be mystified.

— ROGER MARTINEZ

If you have a curious mind like me, "100+ Unexplained Mysteries for Curious Minds" is a must-read. From UFOs to lost civilizations, this book has a bit of everything. The author, Luke Marsh, definitely did his homework. The narratives are intriguing and detailed. A fascinating read that keeps you turning the pages. Solid 5 stars!

— CHRISTOFER

I'd like to use this book to plan future vacations to visit many of the places the author talks about! Each section is well written and researched, and I really enjoyed the author's commentary on the psychological and social aspects of the different events throughout the book.

— AMANDA

100+ SPORTS LEGENDS THROUGHOUT HISTORY

100+ SPORTS LEGENDS THROUGHOUT HISTORY

A COLLECTION OF THE GREATEST ATHLETES AND THEIR UNFORGETTABLE ACHIEVEMENTS, IMPACT ON SOCIETY, AND INFLUENCE ON FUTURE GENERATIONS OF ATHLETES

THE ULTIMATE 100 SERIES

LUKE MARSH

Book Bound Studios

Copyright © 2023 by Luke Marsh

All rights reserved. No part of this book may be reproduced, stored in a retrieval system, or transmitted in any form or by any means, electronic, mechanical, photocopying, recording, or otherwise, without the prior written permission of the publisher, Book Bound Studios.

The information contained in this book is based on the author's personal experiences and research. While every effort has been made to ensure the accuracy of the information presented, the author and publisher cannot be held responsible for any errors or omissions.

This book is intended for general informational purposes only and is not a substitute for professional medical, legal, or financial advice. If you have specific questions about any medical, legal, or financial matters, you should consult with a qualified healthcare professional, attorney, or financial advisor.

Book Bound Studios is not affiliated with any product or vendor mentioned in this book. The views expressed in this book are those of the author and do not necessarily reflect the views of Book Bound Studios.

This book is dedicated to all the athletes who have dared to dream, push their limits, and inspire others with their passion and perseverance. To the sports enthusiasts who find joy and inspiration in every game, this is for you. May the stories of these legendary athletes remind us all that anything is possible with hard work, determination, and a love for the game.

It's just a job. Grass grows, birds fly, waves pound the sand. I beat people up.

— MUHAMMAD ALI

CONTENTS

From the Author   xvii
The World of Sports Legends   xix

1. THE PIONEERS: EARLY SPORTS LEGENDS   1
   The Birth of Modern Sports: The 19th Century Pioneers   3
   The Unforgettable Babe Ruth: Baseball's First Superstar   5
   Jesse Owens: Defying Boundaries and Breaking Barriers   6
   The Golden Age of Boxing: Jack Dempsey and Joe Louis   7
   The Rise of Women in Sports: Babe Didrikson Zaharias and Alice Marble   9
   The Emergence of Tennis Legends: Bill Tilden and Suzanne Lenglen   10
   The Original Hockey Heroes: Maurice "Rocket" Richard and Gordie Howe   11
   The Early Days of Football: Jim Thorpe and Red Grange   13
   The Birth of Basketball Legends: George Mikan and Bob Cousy   14
   The Pioneers of Golf: Bobby Jones and Walter Hagen   15
   The Lasting Legacy of Early Sports Legends   17

2. THE GOLDEN AGE OF ATHLETICS: TRACK AND FIELD LEGENDS   19
   The Sprint Kings: Dominating the Short Distances   21
   The Middle-Distance Maestros: A Blend of Speed and Endurance   22
   The Long-Distance Legends: Conquering the Marathon and Beyond   24
   The Hurdle Heroes: Grace and Power Over Barriers   25
   The Vertical Leap: High Jump and Pole Vault Pioneers   27
   The Horizontal Leap: Long Jump and Triple Jump Titans   28
   The Throwing Giants: Shot Put, Discus, Hammer, and Javelin Masters   29
   The Decathlon and Heptathlon: The Ultimate Test of Athleticism   31

The Trailblazers: Breaking Barriers and Shattering Records	32
The Legacy: How Track and Field Legends Inspired Future Generations	34
The Enduring Impact of the Golden Age of Athletics	35

3. THE BEAUTIFUL GAME: SOCCER LEGENDS ... 39

The Pioneers: Early Soccer Legends Who Shaped the Game	41
Goalkeepers: The Last Line of Defense and Their Unforgettable Saves	42
Defenders: The Art of Stopping Goals and Building Attacks	44
Midfield Maestros: The Playmakers Who Controlled the Game	45
Strikers: The Goal-Scoring Machines and Their Legendary Moments	47
The Managers: Masterminds Behind the Success of Soccer Legends	48
Rivalries and Partnerships: The Duels and Bonds That Defined Careers	50
The World Stage: Unforgettable Performances in International Tournaments	51
Breaking Barriers: Soccer Legends Who Transcended the Sport	53
The Future: Rising Stars and the Next Generation of Soccer Legends	54
The Enduring Legacy of Soccer's Greatest Legends	55

4. THE COURT KINGS: BASKETBALL LEGENDS ... 59

The Pioneers: Early Legends Who Shaped the Sport	61
High-Flying Dunkers: The Aerial Artists of Basketball	62
The Playmakers: Point Guards Who Defined the Game	64
Sharpshooters: The Greatest Shooters in Basketball History	65
The Big Men: Dominant Centers and Power Forwards	67
The Two-Way Stars: Legends Known for Their Offensive and Defensive Prowess	68
International Icons: The Global Impact of Basketball Legends	70
The Coaches: Masterminds Behind the Success of Basketball Greats	71

Record Breakers: Unforgettable Achievements and Milestones	73
The Legacy: How Basketball Legends Inspire Future Generations	74
The Enduring Impact of the Court Kings	76
5. THE GRIDIRON GREATS: FOOTBALL LEGENDS	79
The Quarterback Kings: Masterminds of the Game	81
The Running Back Revolution: Speed and Power Unleashed	82
Wide Receivers: The Art of the Impossible Catch	84
The Offensive Line: Unsung Heroes of the Gridiron	85
The Defensive Line: The Wall of Intimidation	86
Linebackers: The Heart and Soul of the Defense	88
The Secondary: The Last Line of Defense	89
Special Teams: The Game Changers	90
The Coaches: Architects of Gridiron Greatness	92
The Most Memorable Moments in Football History	93
The Enduring Legacy of Football Legends	95
6. THE ICE WARRIORS: HOCKEY LEGENDS	97
The Pioneers: Early Hockey Heroes	99
The Golden Era: Hockey's Most Dominant Players	101
The Goalie Greats: Masters of the Crease	102
The Defensemen: Guardians of the Blue Line	104
The Playmakers: Architects of the Game	105
The Snipers: Scoring Machines on Ice	106
The Enforcers: Hockey's Toughest Competitors	108
The Captains: Leaders of Legendary Teams	109
The Coaches: Visionaries Behind the Bench	111
The International Stage: Hockey Legends Around the World	112
The Enduring Legacy of Hockey's Greatest Players	114
7. THE DIAMOND STARS: BASEBALL LEGENDS	117
The Early Pioneers: Setting the Stage for Baseball's Golden Age	119
The Power Hitters: Home Run Kings Who Captivated Fans	120
The Pitching Phenoms: Dominant Arms on the Mound	121
The Speed Demons: Base Stealers and Defensive Wizards	123

The Iron Men: Record-Breaking Streaks and Longevity in the Game	124
The Barrier Breakers: Pioneers of Integration and Inclusion	126
The Managers and Coaches: Masterminds Behind the Success	127
The Unsung Heroes: Overlooked Legends Who Made Their Mark	129
The Modern Era: Baseball Stars Shining Bright in the 21st Century	130
The Legacy: How Baseball Legends Continue to Inspire Future Generations	132
The Enduring Impact of Baseball's Greatest Legends	133

8. THE RACQUET MASTERS: TENNIS LEGENDS	135
The Golden Era: Tennis Legends of the Early 20th Century	137
The Swinging Sixties: Tennis Icons Who Defined the Decade	138
The Battle of the Sexes: Pioneering Female Tennis Legends	140
The Rivalries: Epic Clashes Between Tennis Titans	142
The Modern Masters: Tennis Legends of the 21st Century	143
The Record Breakers: Tennis Players Who Made History	145
The Style Icons: Tennis Legends Who Transformed the Sport's Fashion	146
The Inspirational Stories: Overcoming Adversity on the Tennis Court	148
The Future of Tennis: Up-and-Coming Players to Watch	150
The Legacy: How Tennis Legends Have Shaped the Sport	151
The Enduring Impact of Tennis Legends on the Game	153

9. THE SWEET SCIENCE: BOXING LEGENDS	155
The Golden Age of Boxing: Pioneers and Innovators	157
Heavyweight Heroes: The Titans of the Ring	159
Middleweight Masters: The Perfect Balance of Power and Speed	160
Welterweight Warriors: The Fierce Competitors of a Storied Division	162
Lightweight Legends: The Fast and the Furious	163

The Women of Boxing: Breaking Barriers and Making History	165
The Greatest Rivalries: Epic Battles That Defined the Sport	166
The Trainers and Mentors: The Architects Behind the Legends	168
The Cultural Impact of Boxing: How the Sweet Science Shaped Society	169
The Future of Boxing: Rising Stars and the Evolution of the Sport	171
The Enduring Legacy of Boxing's Greatest Legends	172
10. THE ULTIMATE COMPETITORS: LEGENDS FROM VARIOUS SPORTS	175
The Titans of Tennis: Unmatched Skill and Passion	177
Basketball's Greatest: Soaring to New Heights	178
Soccer Superstars: Masters of the Beautiful Game	179
The Giants of Golf: Swinging Their Way to Success	181
Track and Field Legends: Speed, Strength, and Endurance	182
Swimming Sensations: Making Waves in the Pool	184
Boxing's Best: The Art of the Knockout	185
The Heroes of Hockey: Ice-Cold Precision and Power	186
The Pioneers of Extreme Sports: Defying Gravity and Fear	188
The Champions of the Paralympics: Inspiring Stories of Triumph	189
The Enduring Legacy of Various Sports Legends	191
The Enduring Legacy of Sports Legends	193
About the Author	201
From the Author	203

$10.99 FREE EBOOK

Receive Your Free Copy of 100+ Interesting Real Stories

Or visit:
bookboundstudios.wixsite.com/luke-marsh

THE WORLD OF SPORTS LEGENDS

Throughout the ages, the world has been graced with exceptional individuals who have left an indelible mark on sports. These extraordinary athletes have pushed the boundaries of human potential and inspired generations of fans with their unwavering dedication, passion, and resilience. They are the titans of their respective fields, who have risen above the rest to etch their names in the annals of history. It is with great honor and excitement that we unveil the pantheon of sports legends, a collection of one hundred remarkable stories that celebrate the triumphs and tribulations of these iconic figures.

From the ancient Olympic Games to the modern-day stadiums, the world of sports has always been a stage for the most exceptional talents to showcase their prowess and captivate the hearts of millions. These legends have transcended the boundaries of their sports, becoming symbols of excellence and embodiments of the human spirit. They have defied the odds, shattered records, and redefined the limits of what is possible, leaving behind a legacy that continues to inspire and shape the future of sports.

As we embark on this journey through the world of sports legends, we invite you to join us in celebrating the lives and achievements of these extraordinary individuals. Through their stories, we will explore the depths of their passion, the heights of their accomplishments, and the indomitable spirit that has propelled them to greatness. Together, we will delve into the rich tapestry of sports history, uncovering the moments that have defined these legends and their impact on the world around them.

So, let us begin our voyage into the pantheon of sports legends, where we will discover the tales of courage, determination, and excellence that have shaped the world of sports as we know it today. As we turn the pages of this book, we hope to ignite within you the same passion and admiration for these legends that have fueled our lifelong love affair with the world of sports and its heroes.

Exploring the Wide World of Sports Legends

In this book, we embark on an exciting journey to explore the wide world of sports legends, delving into the lives and achievements of 100+ exceptional athletes who have left an indelible mark on the world of sports. Our expedition will traverse the vast landscape of athletic disciplines, from the adrenaline-pumping action of football, basketball, and soccer, to the elegance and precision of gymnastics, figure skating, and tennis. We will also venture into lesser-known sports, unearthing the stories of legends who have excelled in archery, curling, and chess.

As we navigate the annals of sports history, we will encounter athletes who have defied the odds, shattered records, and inspired generations with incredible feats of strength, speed, and skill. We will celebrate the trailblazers who have broken barriers, transcended cultural boundaries, and paved the way for future generations of athletes to follow in their footsteps. Our exploration will not be limited by geographical borders or time periods; we will delve into the lives of legends from all corners of the globe and various eras, showcasing the rich tapestry of human achievement in the world of sports.

In each chapter, we will delve into the life and career of a sports legend, examining their early beginnings, their rise to prominence, and the defining moments that have etched their names into the annals of sports history. We will also explore the impact these athletes have had on their respective sports and the broader cultural and societal implications of their achievements. Through captivating storytelling and meticulous research, we will bring to life the stories of these remarkable individuals, offering readers a unique and intimate glimpse into the world of sports legends.

It is important to note that the selection of the 100+ sports legends featured in this book is by no means an exhaustive or definitive list. The world of sports is vast and ever-evolving, and countless athletes have significantly contributed to their respective disciplines. However, the athletes chosen for this book represent a diverse and inspiring cross-section of the most exceptional and influential figures in the world of sports. We aim to celebrate their achievements, share their stories, and inspire readers to appreciate the incredible impact that sports legends have had on our lives.

As we embark on this thrilling journey through the world of sports legends, we invite you, the reader, to join us in celebrating the extraordinary achievements of these remarkable athletes. Together, we will explore the wide world of sports legends, uncovering the stories of triumph, perseverance, and passion that have shaped the landscape of sports as we know it today.

1
THE PIONEERS: EARLY SPORTS LEGENDS

Ancient Olympic Games in Greece

Throughout history, sports have played a significant role in shaping societies, cultures, and the lives of countless individuals. From the ancient Olympic Games in Greece to the gladiatorial contests of Rome, athletic competition has long been a source of inspiration, entertainment, and camaraderie. As the world evolved, so too did the realm of sports, giving rise to a new breed of athletes who would become legends in their own right. These pioneers of the sporting world excelled in their respective disciplines. They transcended the boundaries of their sports, leaving an indelible mark on the hearts and minds of fans and fellow athletes alike.

The dawn of sports legends can be traced back to the 19th century when modern sports began to take shape and capture the imagination of the masses. This era saw the birth of organized baseball, football, basketball, and many other sports that we know and love today. During this time, the first true sports superstars emerged, captivating audiences with incredible athleticism, skill, and determination.

In this chapter, we will delve into the lives and accomplishments of some of the most iconic pioneers in the world of sports. From the unforgettable Babe Ruth, who revolutionized the game of baseball and became a symbol of American culture, to Jesse Owens, who defied racial barriers and shattered world records on the track, these early sports legends laid the foundation for generations of athletes to follow.

We will also explore the golden age of boxing when titans like Jack Dempsey and Joe Louis ruled the ring and captured the imagination of fans around the world. Additionally, we will examine the rise of women in sports, as trailblazers like Babe Didrikson Zaharias and Alice Marble broke down barriers and proved that female athletes could compete at the highest level.

Furthermore, we will look at the emergence of tennis legends Bill Tilden and Suzanne Lenglen, who brought grace and style to the sport, and the original hockey heroes Maurice "Rocket" Richard and Gordie Howe, who dazzled fans with their skill and tenacity on the ice. We will also delve into the early days of football and basketball, highlighting the contributions of pioneers like Jim Thorpe, Red Grange, George Mikan, and Bob Cousy.

Finally, we will pay tribute to the pioneers of golf, Bobby Jones and Walter Hagen, who elevated the sport to new heights and inspired countless players to take up the game. As we journey through the lives and achievements of these early sports legends, we will gain a deeper appreciation for their lasting impact on the world of sports and the enduring legacy they have left behind.

The Birth of Modern Sports: The 19th Century Pioneers

As the world transitioned into the 19th century, a new era of sports was born. This period saw the emergence of modern sports, with standardized rules and organized competitions becoming more prevalent. The pioneers of this era laid the foundation for the sports legends we know and admire today. Their passion, dedication, and groundbreaking achievements shaped the sports they played and inspired generations of athletes to follow in their footsteps.

The 19th century was a time of rapid industrialization and urbanization, leading to significant societal changes. As people moved from rural areas to cities, they sought new forms of entertainment and leisure activities. As a result, sports, which had previously been informal and localized, began to evolve into more organized and structured events. This transformation was driven by establishing clubs, associations, and governing bodies that sought to standardize rules and promote fair competition.

One of the earliest pioneers of modern sports was William Webb Ellis, an Englishman credited with inventing rugby in 1823. Legend has it that during a football game at Rugby School, Ellis picked up the ball and ran with it, creating a new sport that combined elements of football and wrestling. This innovation led to the formation of the Rugby Football Union in 1871, which established the first standardized rules for the game.

In cricket, W.G. Grace was a towering figure who dominated the sport during the latter half of the 19th century. Known for his exceptional batting skills and charismatic personality, Grace was instrumental in popularizing cricket and elevating it to a professional level. His remarkable career spanned over four decades, during which he set numerous records and became the first player to score 100 first-class centuries.

The 19th century also witnessed the birth of modern football with the establishment of the English Football Association in 1863. This organization was responsible for creating the first standardized rules of the game, which laid the groundwork for the sport's global popularity. Early football pioneers like Charles W. Alcock and Arthur Kinnaird played crucial roles in organizing the first international matches and promoting the sport across the British Empire.

Across the Atlantic, the United States saw the emergence of baseball as a national pastime. Alexander Cartwright, often referred to as the "father of baseball," developed the modern rules of the game in the 1840s. His innovations, such as the diamond-shaped field and the three-strike rule, transformed baseball into a more organized and spectator-friendly sport. The formation of the National Association of Base Ball Players in 1857 further solidified baseball's status as a popular American sport.

The 19th century was also when women began to make their mark in the world of sports. Despite facing numerous societal barriers, female pioneers such as Lottie Dod and Charlotte Cooper defied expectations and achieved remarkable success in tennis. Their victories in the early Wimbledon Championships paved the way for future generations of female athletes to compete on an equal footing with their male counterparts.

In conclusion, the 19th century was a pivotal period in sports history, marked by the birth of modern games and the emergence of legendary pioneers. These early sports heroes revolutionized their respective disciplines and inspired countless athletes to pursue their dreams and strive for greatness. Their lasting legacy continues to shape the world of sports today as we celebrate and honor the achievements of the legends who followed in their footsteps.

The Unforgettable Babe Ruth: Baseball's First Superstar

In the annals of sports history, few names evoke as much reverence and awe as that of Babe Ruth. Born George Herman Ruth Jr. on February 6, 1895, in Baltimore, Maryland, the man known as the "Sultan of Swat" and "The Bambino" was destined to leave an indelible mark on the world of baseball and become its first true superstar.

Ruth's journey to baseball stardom began at a young age when he was sent to St. Mary's Industrial School for Boys, a reform school and orphanage. Here, he honed his skills under the tutelage of Brother Matthias Boutlier, who recognized Ruth's prodigious talent and helped him develop into a formidable player. Ruth's exceptional abilities as both a pitcher and a hitter soon caught the attention of Jack Dunn, the owner of the Baltimore Orioles, a minor league team. Dunn signed Ruth to his first professional contract in 1914, and during this time, he acquired the nickname "Babe."

Ruth's meteoric rise through the ranks of professional baseball was nothing short of astonishing. After a brief stint with the Orioles, he was sold to the Boston Red Sox, where he made his major league debut as a pitcher. Ruth quickly established himself as one of the best pitchers in the league, but his prowess at the plate would ultimately define his career.

In 1919, Ruth was sold to the New York Yankees, a move that would change the course of baseball history. With the Yankees, Ruth transitioned from a pitcher to an outfielder, allowing him to focus on his hitting. And hit, he did. Ruth's mighty swing and uncanny ability to hit home runs captivated fans and propelled the Yankees to new heights. He led the league in home runs for ten seasons and held the record for the most home runs in a single season (60) until it was broken by Roger Maris in 1961.

Babe Ruth's impact on the game of baseball cannot be overstated. He revolutionized the sport, ushering in the era of the home run and transforming it from a game of strategy and small ball to one of power and spectacle. In addition, his larger-than-life personality and penchant for theatrics on and off the field made him a beloved figure among fans and helped popularize the sport nationwide.

Ruth's legendary career ended in 1935 when he retired as a member of the Boston Braves. However, his incredible achievements on the field, including 714 career home runs, a .342 batting average, and seven World Series titles, earned him a well-deserved place in the Baseball Hall of Fame in 1936 as part of its inaugural class.

The legacy of Babe Ruth extends far beyond his impressive statistics and accolades. He pioneered the world of sports, transcending the game of baseball and becoming a cultural icon. His charisma, talent, and love for the game continue to inspire generations of athletes and fans alike, solidifying his status as one of the most unforgettable legends in sports history.

Jesse Owens: Defying Boundaries and Breaking Barriers

In the annals of sports history, few athletes have left as indelible a mark as Jesse Owens. Born in 1913 in Oakville, Alabama, Owens overcame the challenges of poverty and racial discrimination to become one of the most celebrated and revered athletes of the 20th century. His incredible achievements on the track shattered records and broke barriers, defying the boundaries of race, politics, and social expectations.

Jesse Owens first rose to prominence as a high school track star in Cleveland, Ohio, where his family had moved in search of a better life. However, his exceptional talent was evident from an early age, and he soon caught the attention of college coaches. Owens chose to attend Ohio State University, where he excelled in track and field, setting numerous records and earning the nickname "The Buckeye Bullet."

However, at the 1936 Berlin Olympics, Owens truly cemented his status as a sports legend. In a world still reeling from the Great Depression and on the brink of World War II, the Berlin Games were intended by Adolf Hitler to showcase the superiority of the Aryan race. Owens, an African American, defied Hitler's racist ideology by winning four gold medals in the 100 meters, 200 meters, long jump, and 4x100-meter relay. His victories were a powerful statement against racial prejudice and a testament to the power of sports to unite people across cultural and political divides.

Owens' success in Berlin was a triumph for African Americans and a significant milestone in the broader struggle for civil rights. His victories demonstrated that black athletes could compete at the highest level and helped pave the way for future generations of African American sports stars. Owens' achievements also catalyzed change within the United States, challenging the deeply ingrained racial prejudices of the time and inspiring countless others to follow in his footsteps.

Despite his monumental accomplishments, Owens faced significant challenges upon returning to the United States. He struggled to find work and was often treated as a second-class citizen due to the color of his skin. However, Owens remained committed to using his platform to promote equality and social change. He dedicated much of his life to working with underprivileged youth and advocating for civil rights, leaving a lasting legacy on and off the track.

In conclusion, Jesse Owens' incredible achievements as an athlete and his unwavering commitment to social justice make him a true pioneer in sports. His victories in the face of adversity continue to inspire athletes and activists alike, reminding us of the power of sports to transcend boundaries and break down barriers. As we celebrate the early legends of sports, we must remember the courage and determination of Jesse Owens, whose impact on the world of sports and society as a whole will never be forgotten.

The Golden Age of Boxing: Jack Dempsey and Joe Louis

The Golden Age of Boxing, from the 1920s to the 1950s, was when boxing reached new heights in popularity and produced some of the most iconic and memorable fighters in history. Jack Dempsey and Joe Louis, two of the most prominent figures of this era, whose incredible skill, determination, and charisma captivated audiences and left an indelible mark on the sport.

Jack Dempsey, born William Harrison Dempsey in 1895, was a force to be reckoned with in the boxing world. Known as the "Manassa

Mauler," Dempsey's aggressive and relentless fighting style made him a fan favorite and a formidable opponent. He began his professional boxing career in 1914, and by 1919, he had earned a shot at the world heavyweight title against Jess Willard. In a stunning upset, Dempsey defeated Willard in just three rounds, becoming the new heavyweight champion of the world.

Dempsey's reign as champion lasted from 1919 to 1926, during which he successfully defended his title five times. His most famous bout was the "Battle of the Century" against Georges Carpentier in 1921, the first boxing match to generate over a million dollars in revenue. Dempsey's charisma and exciting fighting style made him a household name and helped popularize boxing.

Joe Louis, born Joseph Louis Barrow in 1914, was another legendary figure of the Golden Age of Boxing. Known as the "Brown Bomber," Louis was a powerful and skilled fighter who dominated the heavyweight division for over a decade. He began his professional career in 1934, and by 1937, he had earned a shot at the world heavyweight title against James J. Braddock. Louis defeated Braddock in eight rounds, becoming the new heavyweight champion of the world.

Louis's reign as champion lasted from 1937 to 1949, during which he successfully defended his title a record 25 times. One of his most famous bouts was the 1938 rematch against German fighter Max Schmeling, who had previously handed Louis his first professional loss. In a highly anticipated and politically charged match, Louis defeated Schmeling in just two minutes and four seconds, solidifying his status as a national hero and symbol of American strength.

Jack Dempsey and Joe Louis were trailblazers in boxing, transcending the sport and becoming cultural icons. Their incredible skill, determination, and charisma captivated audiences and inspired future generations of fighters. The Golden Age of Boxing was when the sport reached new heights in popularity, and the legacy of these early sports legends continues to shape the world of boxing today.

The Rise of Women in Sports: Babe Didrikson Zaharias and Alice Marble

The early 20th century marked a significant turning point in sports as women began to make their mark and shatter the glass ceiling that had long confined them to the sidelines. Two trailblazing women, Babe Didrikson Zaharias, and Alice Marble, emerged as pioneers in their respective sports, inspiring generations of female athletes to follow in their footsteps.

Babe Didrikson Zaharias, born in 1911, was a true all-around athlete who excelled in multiple sports, including basketball, track and field, and golf. Her incredible talent and determination were evident from a young age, as she led her high school basketball team to a state championship and set multiple world records in track and field events. However, Zaharias' most notable achievements came in the sport of golf. She won 41 LPGA Tour events, including ten major championships, and was a founding Ladies Professional Golf Association (LPGA) member. Her dominance on the golf course was so profound that she became the first woman to compete in a men's PGA Tour event, further solidifying her status as a trailblazer in women's sports.

Alice Marble, born in 1913, was a tennis prodigy who stormed the sport in the late 1930s. Known for her powerful serve and aggressive net play, Marble quickly rose through the ranks and became the top-ranked American female tennis player by 1936. Her illustrious career included winning 18 Grand Slam titles, including five singles championships at Wimbledon and the U.S. Open. Marble's impact on the sport extended beyond her on-court accomplishments, as she strongly advocated for equal pay and opportunities for female athletes. She even played a pivotal role in breaking the color barrier in tennis, lobbying for the inclusion of African-American tennis star Althea Gibson in major tournaments.

Babe Didrikson Zaharias and Alice Marble faced numerous challenges and prejudices in pursuing athletic excellence. Still, their unwavering determination and passion for their respective sports allowed them to overcome these obstacles and pave the way for future generations of female athletes. Their groundbreaking achievements challenged societal norms and expectations and demonstrated that women were just as capable of excelling in sports as their male counterparts.

In conclusion, the rise of women in sports during the early 20th century was marked by the incredible accomplishments of pioneers like Babe Didrikson Zaharias and Alice Marble. Their determination, talent, and advocacy for equality in sports have left a lasting legacy that inspires and empowers female athletes today. As we celebrate the achievements of these early sports legends, we must also recognize the importance of continuing to support and uplift the women who are breaking barriers and making history in the world of sports today.

The Emergence of Tennis Legends: Bill Tilden and Suzanne Lenglen

As the world of sports continued to evolve and expand, tennis emerged as a popular and competitive game that attracted exceptional athletes. Two of the earliest and most influential tennis legends were Bill Tilden and Suzanne Lenglen, who not only dominated the sport during their time but also left an indelible mark on the history of tennis.

Bill Tilden, born in 1893 in Philadelphia, was an American tennis player who revolutionized the sport with his powerful and precise playing style. Known as "Big Bill," Tilden was a force to be reckoned with on the court. He won 10 Grand Slam singles titles, including seven U.S. Championships (now known as the U.S. Open) and three Wimbledon titles. Tilden was also a member of the victorious United States Davis Cup team for seven consecutive years, from 1920 to 1926.

Tilden's impact on the sport went beyond his impressive list of titles. He was a true innovator, introducing new techniques and strategies that would shape the future of tennis. His powerful serve and aggressive net play were considered groundbreaking, and his tactical approach to the game influenced generations of players. Tilden's charisma and flamboyant personality also helped to popularize tennis and bring it to a broader audience.

On the other side of the Atlantic, Suzanne Lenglen was making her mark as one of the first female tennis superstars. Born in France in 1899, Lenglen was a trailblazer for women in sports, breaking down barriers and challenging societal norms. She won 21 Grand Slam titles, including six Wimbledon singles titles and eight World Hard Court Championships. Lenglen's rivalry with American player Helen Wills Moody was legendary, and their matches were highly anticipated events that captivated audiences worldwide.

Lenglen's impact on tennis was more expansive than just her on-court success. She pioneered women's sports, pushing for equal recognition and opportunities for female athletes. Lenglen's bold and daring playing style, coupled with her fashionable and flamboyant on-court attire, challenged the conservative norms of the time and paved the way for future generations of female athletes. She was also instrumental in popularizing the sport in Europe, particularly in her home country of France.

The legacies of Bill Tilden and Suzanne Lenglen continue to resonate in the world of tennis today. Their innovative playing styles, tactical approaches, and larger-than-life personalities helped to shape the sport into what it is today. As pioneers in their respective fields, Tilden and Lenglen set the stage for future tennis legends and played a crucial role in the development and popularization of the sport as a whole. Their contributions to tennis will forever be remembered and celebrated as the sport continues to evolve and produce new legends.

The Original Hockey Heroes: Maurice "Rocket" Richard and Gordie Howe

Numerous legends have graced the world of ice hockey, but none have left a more indelible mark on the sport than Maurice "Rocket" Richard and Gordie Howe. These two extraordinary players revolutionized the game with their exceptional skills and passion and inspired generations of future hockey stars. In this section, we will delve into the lives and careers of these two original hockey heroes, exploring their incredible achievements and their lasting impact on the sport.

Born in Montreal, Quebec, in 1921, Maurice Richard was destined for greatness from a young age. His passion for hockey was evident as he honed his skills on his neighborhood's frozen ponds and makeshift rinks. Richard's exceptional talent was soon recognized, and he made his NHL debut for the Montreal Canadiens in 1942.

Richard's nickname, "Rocket," was a testament to his incredible speed and powerful shot. He was the first player in NHL history to score 50 goals in a single season, achieving this remarkable feat in just 50 games during the 1944-45 season. This record stood for nearly four decades until it was broken by Wayne Gretzky in 1981.

Throughout his illustrious career, Richard won the Hart Trophy as the league's most valuable player and led the Canadiens to eight Stanley Cup championships. He was also the first player to reach the 500-goal milestone, finishing his career with a total of 544 goals. Richard's fiery spirit and unwavering determination made him a fan favorite and a symbol of French-Canadian pride.

Gordie Howe's incredible career spanned five decades, earning him the nickname "Mr. Hockey." Born in Floral, Saskatchewan, in 1928, Howe's humble beginnings did not deter him from pursuing his sports passion. He made his NHL debut for the Detroit Red Wings in 1946, and it wasn't long before he established himself as one of the league's premier players.

Howe's versatility and all-around skill set made him a force to be reckoned with on the ice. He could score goals, set up plays, and even drop the gloves when necessary. This unique combination of talents led to the "Gordie Howe hat trick," which consists of a goal, an assist, and a fight in a single game.

Throughout his remarkable career, Howe won six Hart Trophies as the league's most valuable player and led the Red Wings to four Stanley Cup championships. He held numerous records, including most career goals (801), most career points (1,850), and most games played (1,767) until Wayne Gretzky eventually surpassed them.

Maurice "Rocket" Richard and Gordie Howe's contributions to hockey cannot be overstated. Their exceptional talent, passion, and dedication to the game have left a lasting impact on the sport and inspired countless players who have followed in their footsteps. As game pioneers, their names will forever be etched in the annals of hockey history. Their legendary status will continue to be celebrated by fans and players alike.

The Early Days of Football: Jim Thorpe and Red Grange

As we delve into the early days of football, two names stand out as pioneers who shaped the sport and captured the hearts of fans across America: Jim Thorpe and Red Grange. These two legends showcased their incredible athletic abilities on the field and played a crucial role in popularizing football and transforming it into the beloved sport we know today.

Jim Thorpe, a Native American from the Sac and Fox Nation, was a true all-around athlete who excelled in multiple sports, including track and field, baseball, and football. Born in 1887, Thorpe's journey to football stardom began at the Carlisle Indian Industrial School in Pennsylvania, where he played under the guidance of legendary coach Glenn "Pop" Warner. Thorpe's incredible speed, strength, and agility quickly made him a standout player, and in 1912, he led Carlisle to a national championship victory.

Thorpe's prowess on the football field was matched only by his achievements in track and field. At the 1912 Stockholm Olympics, he won gold medals in both the pentathlon and decathlon, earning him the title "World's Greatest Athlete" from King Gustav V of Sweden. Despite facing numerous challenges and discrimination throughout his life, Thorpe's undeniable talent and determination allowed him to break barriers and become a symbol of hope and inspiration for Native Americans and sports fans.

While Jim Thorpe was a trailblazer for football in the early 20th century, Harold "Red" Grange truly brought the sport into the mainstream. Born in 1903, Grange was nicknamed "The Galloping Ghost" for his incredible speed and elusive running style. As a halfback for the University of Illinois, Grange became a national sensation in 1924 when he scored four touchdowns in just twelve minutes against the University of Michigan, one of the most dominant teams of the era.

Grange's popularity skyrocketed, and he soon became one of the first football players to turn professional, signing with the Chicago Bears in 1925. His decision to go pro was a turning point for the sport, as it helped legitimize professional football and drew massive crowds to games. Grange's barnstorming tours with the Bears, in which they traveled across the country playing exhibition games, were instrumental in spreading the popularity of football and establishing the National Football League (NFL) as a major sports organization.

Both Jim Thorpe and Red Grange left indelible marks on football, paving the way for future generations of players and fans. Their incredible athletic abilities and determination to overcome obstacles and break down barriers have solidified their status as true pioneers of the sport. As we continue to celebrate the achievements of sports legends, it is essential to remember and honor the lasting legacy of these early football heroes.

The Birth of Basketball Legends: George Mikan and Bob Cousy

As basketball began to gain popularity in the early 20th century, it was only a matter of time before legends emerged to captivate fans and set the standard for future generations. Two such pioneers were George Mikan and Bob Cousy, who dominated the game during their respective eras and helped shape the sport into what it is today.

George Mikan, often called "Mr. Basketball," was a towering figure, literally and figuratively. Standing at 6 feet 10 inches, Mikan was a force to be reckoned with on the court. His height and skill set was unprecedented then, and he quickly became a dominant center in the early years of professional basketball. Mikan's career began in the 1940s, playing for the Chicago American Gears before joining the Minneapolis Lakers in the newly-formed Basketball Association of America (BAA), which later became the NBA.

Mikan's impact on the game was immense. He was a scoring machine, leading the league in scoring for three consecutive seasons and becoming the first player to score over 10,000 points in his career. His signature move, the hook shot, became a staple for big men in the years to come. Mikan's dominance in the paint also led to several rule changes, including the goaltending rule and the lane widening to prevent him from camping near the basket. His success with the Lakers, winning five championships, solidified his status as one of the game's first true superstars.

While Mikan revolutionized the center position, Bob Cousy did the same for the point guard role. Known as "The Houdini of the Hardwood," Cousy's dazzling ball-handling skills and court vision were unlike anything the basketball world had seen. Cousy began his career with the Boston Celtics in 1950 and quickly became the team's floor general, leading the league in assists for eight consecutive seasons.

Cousy's impact on the game went beyond his impressive statistics. He pioneered in bringing flair and creativity to the sport, with his no-look passes and behind-the-back dribbles becoming legend. Cousy's style of play was instrumental in making basketball a more entertaining and engaging sport for fans, and his influence can still be seen in the flashy playmaking of today's point guards.

George Mikan and Bob Cousy laid the foundation for the modern basketball game. Their skill, innovation, and passion for the sport earned them individual accolades and championships and inspired countless future legends to follow in their footsteps. As we continue to marvel at the feats of today's basketball superstars, it is essential to remember and appreciate the pioneers who paved the way for their success.

The Pioneers of Golf: Bobby Jones and Walter Hagen

The sport of golf has a rich history, dating back to 15th-century Scotland. However, in the early 20th century, the game truly began to capture the imagination of sports enthusiasts worldwide. Two men, in particular, played a significant role in popularizing golf and establishing it as a major sport: Bobby Jones and Walter Hagen. These pioneers dominated the game during their respective careers and left an indelible mark on the sport that continues to be felt today.

Bobby Jones, born in 1902 in Atlanta, Georgia, was a golf prodigy who displayed an extraordinary talent for the game from a young age. Despite never turning professional, Jones achieved remarkable success in the sport, winning 13 major championships between 1923 and 1930. However, his most significant accomplishment came in 1930 when he won the Grand Slam, a feat that had never been achieved before and has only been matched once. Jones' Grand Slam consisted of winning the U.S. Open, the British Open, the U.S. Amateur, and the British Amateur championships in a calendar year.

Jones' success on the golf course was matched by his impact off it. He was instrumental in founding the Augusta National Golf Club and creating the Masters Tournament, which has become one of the most prestigious events in the sport. Jones' sportsmanship, humility, and dedication to the game earned him widespread admiration and respect, and he remains an iconic figure in golf.

Walter Hagen, born in 1892 in Rochester, New York, was another trailblazer in the early days of golf. Hagen turned professional at age 20 and went on to win 11 major championships, making him one of the most successful golfers of all time. Known for his flamboyant personality and stylish attire, Hagen was a true showman who brought a sense of glamour and excitement to the sport.

Hagen's impact on golf extended beyond his success on the course. He was a tireless advocate for the rights of professional golfers, helping to break down the barriers between amateurs and professionals at the time. Hagen's efforts played a crucial role in elevating the status of professional golfers and paving the way for the lucrative careers enjoyed by today's players.

Both Bobby Jones and Walter Hagen left an indelible mark on the sport of golf, not only through their incredible achievements on the course but also through their contributions to the growth and development of the game. Their pioneering efforts laid the foundation for the modern golf landscape, and their legacies continue to inspire and influence golfers worldwide. As we celebrate the accomplishments of these early sports legends, we are reminded of the enduring impact that pioneers can have on the sports they love.

The Lasting Legacy of Early Sports Legends

As we conclude our journey through the lives and achievements of the pioneers of sports, it is essential to reflect on the legacy these early sports legends left behind. These remarkable individuals revolutionized their respective sports and transcended the boundaries of athleticism, leaving an indelible mark on society and inspiring generations of athletes and fans alike.

The pioneers of sports were trailblazers in every sense of the word. They broke records, shattered stereotypes, and defied expectations, proving that the human spirit can achieve greatness despite adversity. Their stories of perseverance, determination, and resilience continue to inspire and motivate people from all walks of life to strive for excellence and overcome obstacles.

Babe Ruth, Jesse Owens, Jack Dempsey, Joe Louis, Babe Didrikson Zaharias, Alice Marble, Bill Tilden, Suzanne Lenglen, Maurice "Rocket" Richard, Gordie Howe, Jim Thorpe, Red Grange, George Mikan, Bob Cousy, Bobby Jones, and Walter Hagen – these names are synonymous with the birth of modern sports and the rise of sports as a cultural phenomenon. Moreover, they paved the way for future generations of athletes, setting new performance standards and redefining what it meant to be a sports legend.

The early sports legends also played a crucial role in breaking down social barriers and promoting inclusivity in sports. Figures like Jesse Owens and Joe Louis challenged racial prejudices. At the same time, Babe Didrikson Zaharias and Alice Marble proved that women could excel in sports just as much as their male counterparts. These pioneers changed the face of sports and contributed to the broader struggle for equality and social justice.

Moreover, the early sports legends helped popularize and globalize their respective sports, turning them into the massive industries they are today. These athletes' feats captured the imaginations of millions, turning sports into a universal language that transcended national, cultural, and linguistic barriers. Their influence can still be felt today, as sports unite people from all around the globe.

In conclusion, the lasting legacy of the early sports legends is evident in the countless records they set, the barriers they broke, and the lives they touched. Their stories of triumph and perseverance continue to inspire athletes and fans alike, reminding us of the power of sports to uplift, unite, and transform. As we celebrate the achievements of these pioneers, we also look forward to the future, eagerly anticipating the next generation of sports legends who will carry on their legacy and continue to push the boundaries of human potential.

2
THE GOLDEN AGE OF ATHLETICS: TRACK AND FIELD LEGENDS

Athletics, Track and Field

The world of sports has always been a stage for extraordinary athleticism, strength, and endurance feats. Among the many disciplines that have captured the imagination of fans and athletes alike, track and field hold a special place in the pantheon of sports legends as one of the oldest and most diverse sporting events. As a result, track and field has given rise to some of the most iconic and inspiring figures in sports history. In this chapter, we will delve into the golden age of athletics, exploring the lives and achievements of the legends who have left an indelible mark on the track and field world.

The emergence of track and field legends can be traced back to the ancient Olympic Games, where athletes from various city-states would gather to compete in a range of events, including running, jumping, and throwing. These early competitions laid the foundation for modern sports. As the years went by, new generations of competitors would surpass the feats of these ancient athletes, each pushing the boundaries of human potential.

The golden age of athletics, from the early 20th century to the present day, has seen the rise of numerous track and field legends rise. These athletes have not only shattered records and redefined the limits of human performance, but they have also inspired countless others to pursue their dreams and strive for greatness. From the sprint kings who have dominated short distances to the middle-distance maestros who have blended speed and endurance, these legends have left an indelible mark on the sport and the world.

In this chapter, we will explore the lives and achievements of these track and field legends, delving into their training, their mindset, and the obstacles they overcame to reach the pinnacle of their sport. We will also examine these athletes' impact on the world of track and field, inspiring future generations to push the boundaries of what is possible and to chase their dreams with passion and determination.

As we journey through the golden age of athletics, we will encounter the stories of the sprint kings, the middle-distance maestros, the long-distance legends, the hurdle heroes, the vertical and horizontal leap pioneers, the throwing giants, and the ultimate test of athleticism in the decathlon and heptathlon. We will also tribute the trailblazers who broke barriers and shattered records, leaving a lasting legacy for future generations.

Join us as we celebrate the incredible achievements of these track and field legends, and discover the enduring impact of the golden age of athletics on the world of sports and beyond.

The Sprint Kings: Dominating the Short Distances

The world of athletics has been graced by numerous sprinters who have left an indelible mark on the sport. These "Sprint Kings" have dominated short distances and redefined the limits of human speed. In this section, we will delve into the lives and achievements of these remarkable athletes who have etched their names in track and field history annals.

The first name that comes to mind when discussing sprint legends is the charismatic Usain Bolt. Hailing from Jamaica, Bolt is widely regarded as the fastest man in the world. With his lightning speed and larger-than-life personality, he has captured the imagination of millions. Bolt's incredible achievements include eight Olympic gold medals and eleven World Championship titles. His world records in the 100 meters (9.58 seconds) and 200 meters (19.19 seconds) still stand unchallenged, showcasing his unparalleled dominance in the sport.

Another sprint king who deserves mention is the American athlete Carl Lewis. A versatile and gifted sprinter, Lewis excelled in the 100 meters and 200 meters events and the long jump. Over his illustrious career, he amassed nine Olympic gold medals and eight World Championship titles. Lewis was also the first athlete to break the 10-second barrier in the 100 meters, setting a new standard for speed and power.

The list of sprint kings would only be complete by mentioning the legendary Jesse Owens. Competing in a time when racial discrimination was rampant, Owens defied all odds and emerged as a beacon of hope for millions. At the 1936 Berlin Olympics, he won four gold medals in the 100 meters, 200 meters, long jump, and 4x100 meters relay, shattering Adolf Hitler's myth of Aryan supremacy. Owens' incredible achievements cemented his status as a track and field legend and a powerful symbol of equality and perseverance.

The world of female sprinters has also seen its fair share of legends. Florence Griffith-Joyner, affectionately known as "Flo-Jo," was an American sprinter who took the world by storm with her blistering speed and flamboyant style. She set world records in the 100 meters (10.49 seconds) and 200 meters (21.34 seconds) at the 1988 Seoul Olympics, which still stands today. Her five Olympic medals and five World Championship titles testify to her incredible talent and dedication to the sport.

Another female sprinting legend is the Jamaican athlete Merlene Ottey. Nicknamed the "Queen of the Track," Ottey's career spanned over two decades, during which she won nine Olympic medals and fourteen World Championship medals. Her longevity and consistency in the sport are remarkable, making her one of the greatest sprinters ever.

In conclusion, the Sprint Kings have dominated the short distances and inspired generations of athletes to push the boundaries of human potential. Their incredible achievements testify to the power of hard work, determination, and resilience. As we continue to marvel at their feats, we are reminded of the enduring impact of these track and field legends on the world of athletics.

The Middle-Distance Maestros: A Blend of Speed and Endurance

The middle-distance events in track and field showcase the perfect harmony between speed and endurance. These races, ranging from 800 to 3,000 meters, demand a unique combination of physical prowess, mental fortitude, and tactical acumen. The athletes who excel in these events are often regarded as the epitome of versatility and adaptability. This section will delve into the lives and achievements of some of the most iconic middle-distance maestros who have left an indelible mark on athletics.

One cannot discuss middle-distance legends without mentioning the "Czech Locomotive," Emil Zátopek. A true icon of the sport, Zátopek's incredible achievements include winning the 5,000 meters,

10,000 meters, and the marathon at the 1952 Helsinki Olympics, a feat that remains unmatched today. His strict training regimen and unorthodox running style, characterized by a pained expression and lolling head, made him a symbol of grit and determination.

Another middle-distance legend is the British athlete Sebastian Coe, who dominated the 800 meters and 1,500 meters events in the late 1970s and early 1980s. Coe's fierce rivalry with fellow Briton Steve Ovett captivated the world as they traded world records and Olympic titles. Coe's smooth, elegant running style and tactical brilliance earned him four Olympic medals, including back-to-back golds in the 1,500 meters in 1980 and 1984.

The women's middle-distance events have also witnessed their fair share of extraordinary athletes. One such legend is the "Flying Housewife," Fanny Blankers-Koen of the Netherlands. At the 1948 London Olympics, the 30-year-old mother of two defied societal norms and expectations by winning four gold medals in the 100 meters, 200 meters, 80 meters hurdles, and 4x100 meters relay. Her incredible achievements paved the way for future generations of female athletes.

Another trailblazing middle-distance runner is the Algerian-born Hassiba Boulmerka. At the 1992 Barcelona Olympics, Boulmerka became the first African woman to win an Olympic gold medal in track and field, triumphing in the 1,500 meters. Her victory was a powerful statement against the cultural and religious barriers that often hindered female athletes in her region.

The middle-distance events have also been a stage for athletes who have transcended the sport through activism and advocacy. For example, the American 800 meters runner Wilma Rudolph overcame childhood polio to become the first American woman to win three gold medals in a single Olympics at the 1960 Rome Games. Rudolph's success and her fight against racial segregation in the United States made her a symbol of hope and inspiration for millions.

These middle-distance maestros have not only etched their names in the annals of athletic history but have also inspired countless individuals with their resilience, determination, and unwavering spirit.

Their stories serve as a testament to the power of sports to break barriers, challenge norms, and unite people across the globe.

The Long-Distance Legends: Conquering the Marathon and Beyond

The world of long-distance running has produced some of the most awe-inspiring and memorable moments in athletics history. These legends have conquered the grueling 26.2 miles of the marathon and pushed the boundaries of human endurance in ultra-marathons and other long-distance races. In this section, we will delve into the lives and achievements of the long-distance legends who have left an indelible mark on athletics.

The marathon originated in ancient Greece and has long been a symbol of human perseverance and determination. One of the earliest long-distance legends is Spiridon Louis, a Greek water carrier who won the first modern Olympic marathon in 1896. His victory ignited a passion for marathon running that continues to this day.

In the 20th century, the marathon world witnessed the rise of legends such as Abebe Bikila, an Ethiopian runner who won back-to-back Olympic gold medals in 1960 and 1964, running the first race barefoot. Bikila's triumphs paved the way for the dominance of East African runners in long-distance events, with Kenya and Ethiopia producing many world-class athletes.

Among these East African legends, Haile Gebrselassie is one of the greatest long-distance runners ever. Gebrselassie's incredible career spanned over two decades with two Olympic gold medals, four World Championship titles, and numerous world records in distances ranging from 5,000 meters to the marathon.

The women's marathon has its pantheon of legends, with Joan Benoit Samuelson's groundbreaking victory in the first-ever women's Olympic marathon in 1984 inspiring countless female runners. More recently, Paula Radcliffe of Great Britain set a world record in 2003 that stood for 16 years, showcasing her incredible talent and determination.

Beyond the marathon, ultra-marathon races have given rise to a new breed of long-distance legends. Yiannis Kouros, a Greek-Australian runner, is considered the "Running God" of ultra-marathons, having set numerous world records in races ranging from 100 miles to 1,000 miles. His mental and physical fortitude exemplifies the spirit of long-distance running.

Another ultra-marathon legend is Ann Trason, an American runner who has won the prestigious Western States 100-Mile Endurance Run an astounding 14 times. Her incredible achievements have inspired a generation of female ultra-marathoners to push the limits of human endurance.

The long-distance legends of the Golden Age of Athletics have conquered marathons and ultra-marathons and transcended the sport itself. Their stories of perseverance, dedication, and triumph in adversity continue to inspire athletes and non-athletes alike. As we look back on their incredible achievements, we are reminded of the power of the human spirit and the limitless potential within each of us.

The Hurdle Heroes: Grace and Power Over Barriers

The world of athletics has seen numerous athletes with exceptional talent and skill in various disciplines. The hurdlers hold a special place, showcasing a unique blend of grace and power while overcoming barriers. This section will delve into the lives and achievements of some of the most iconic hurdle heroes who have left an indelible mark on the sport during the Golden Age of Athletics.

Hurdling is a demanding discipline that requires athletes to possess speed, strength, agility, flexibility, and impeccable timing. The ability to maintain rhythm and momentum while clearing hurdles is a testament to the extraordinary skill of these athletes. The Golden Age of Athletics witnessed the rise of several hurdlers who dominated their respective events and inspired future generations with their incredible performances.

One of the most prominent names in the history of hurdling is Edwin Moses, an American athlete who reigned supreme in the 400-meter hurdles. Moses was virtually unbeatable in his prime, with an incredible winning streak of 122 consecutive races spanning nearly a decade. His unique stride pattern and exceptional technique allowed him to easily glide over hurdles, making him a true icon of the sport. Moses' two Olympic gold medals and numerous world records testify to his extraordinary talent and dedication.

Another legendary hurdler who left an indelible mark on the sport is Sally Gunnell, a British athlete specializing in the 400-meter hurdles. Gunnell's incredible achievements include an Olympic gold medal, a World Championship title, and a world record, making her one of the most successful female hurdlers ever. Her fierce determination and relentless pursuit of excellence made her a role model for aspiring athletes worldwide.

The Golden Age of Athletics also witnessed the rise of several other remarkable hurdlers, such as Renaldo Nehemiah, an American athlete who dominated the 110-meter hurdles in the late 1970s and early 1980s. Nehemiah's exceptional speed and flawless technique earned him numerous accolades, including a world record for nearly a decade. His transition to a successful career in professional football further highlighted his incredible athleticism and versatility.

The world of hurdling has also seen trailblazers who broke barriers and shattered stereotypes. One such athlete is Wilma Rudolph, an African-American sprinter, and hurdler who overcame polio to become a three-time Olympic gold medalist. Rudolph's incredible journey from a childhood marked by illness and adversity to the pinnacle of athletic success is a testament to her indomitable spirit and resilience.

In conclusion, the Golden Age of Athletics was a period that witnessed the rise of numerous hurdle heroes who displayed exceptional grace and power over barriers. These athletes dominated their respective events and inspired future generations with their incredible performances and unwavering determination. Their enduring impact on the sport of track and field is a testament to their extraordinary talent and the timeless appeal of hurdling to showcase human athleticism and perseverance.

The Vertical Leap: High Jump and Pole Vault Pioneers

The Golden Age of Athletics witnessed the rise of exceptional athletes who defied gravity and soared to new heights, leaving spectators in awe of their incredible feats. In this section, we delve into the world of high jump and pole vault pioneers, who not only pushed the boundaries of human capabilities but also revolutionized the techniques and strategies employed in these events.

High Jump Heroes

The high jump event has always been fascinating, as athletes combine power, agility, and grace to clear a horizontal bar set at remarkable heights. One of the earliest high jump legends was American athlete Dick Fosbury, who revolutionized the sport with his innovative "Fosbury Flop" technique. By arching his back and twisting his body over the bar, Fosbury achieved greater heights than ever, ultimately winning the gold medal at the 1968 Mexico City Olympics and setting a new Olympic record.

Another high jump pioneer was the charismatic Dwight Stones, a two-time Olympic bronze medalist, and multiple world record holder. Stones was known for his flamboyant personality and relentless pursuit of perfection, which led him to experiment with various techniques and training methods. His dedication to the sport inspired a new generation of high jumpers, including the phenomenal Javier Sotomayor from Cuba. He became the first and only person to clear the 8-foot (2.45 meters) barrier in 1993.

Pole Vault Pioneers

The pole vault event is a thrilling combination of speed, strength, and acrobatics. Athletes sprint down the runway, plant a flexible pole into a box, and catapult themselves over a horizontal bar. One of the earliest pole vault legends was Cornelius Warmerdam, an American athlete who dominated the event in the 1940s. Warmerdam was the first vaulter to clear 15 feet (4.57 meters) and held the world record for 15 years. His innovative training methods and dedication to the sport laid the foundation for future pole vault champions.

Sergey Bubka, a Ukrainian pole vaulter, is arguably the most famous and successful athlete in the event's history. Bubka broke the world record an astounding 35 times during his career and was the first to clear the 6-meter (19 feet 8 inches) barrier. His incredible achievements earned him six consecutive World Championship titles and an Olympic gold medal in 1988. Bubka's explosive speed, strength, and flawless technique set a new standard for the sport and inspired countless athletes to follow in his footsteps.

In conclusion, the high jump and pole vault pioneers of the Golden Age of Athletics achieved remarkable personal success and revolutionized how these events were approached. Their innovative techniques, relentless pursuit of excellence, and unwavering dedication to their respective sports have left an indelible mark on the world of athletics and continue to inspire future generations of athletes to reach for the sky.

The Horizontal Leap: Long Jump and Triple Jump Titans

The world of athletics has witnessed numerous awe-inspiring performances in horizontal leap events, with athletes pushing the boundaries of human capabilities. The long and triple jump events have produced some of the most iconic moments in sports history, showcasing the perfect blend of speed, strength, and agility. This section will delve into the fascinating stories of the Titans who ruled the long jump and triple jump events during the golden age of athletics.

The long jump event has been a part of the Olympic Games since its inception in 1896, and it has produced some of the most memorable moments in track and field history. One of the most iconic figures in the long jump is Jesse Owens, who broke the world record in 1935 and won four gold medals at the 1936 Berlin Olympics. Owens' incredible achievements in the face of racial discrimination and political turmoil have made him a symbol of perseverance and triumph.

Another long jump legend is Bob Beamon, who stunned the world with his record-breaking leap of 8.90 meters at the 1968 Mexico City Olympics. Beamon's jump was so extraordinary that it exceeded the measuring equipment available at the time, and it took officials nearly 20 minutes to confirm the result. His record stood for an astounding 23 years until it was finally broken by Mike Powell in 1991.

The triple jump event, also known as the hop, step, and jump, has been a part of the Olympic program since 1896 for men and 1996 for women. This event requires a unique combination of speed, strength, and coordination, as athletes must execute three distinct phases in a single, fluid motion. One of the most dominant figures in the triple jump is Viktor Saneyev, a Soviet athlete who won three consecutive Olympic gold medals in 1968, 1972, and 1976. Saneyev's incredible consistency and longevity in the sport have made him a true icon of the triple jump.

The golden age of athletics also saw the rise of female triple jumpers, with athletes like Inessa Kravets making their mark on the sport. Kravets, a Ukrainian athlete, set the current world record of 15.50 meters at the 1995 World Championships in Gothenburg, Sweden. Her record remains unbroken today, a testament to her extraordinary talent and skill.

The horizontal leap events have produced some of the most captivating moments in athletics history, with athletes defying gravity and pushing the limits of human potential. The long jump and triple jump titans of the golden age have left an indelible mark on the sport, inspiring future generations to dream big and strive for greatness. Their stories of perseverance, determination, and triumph resonate with athletes and fans alike, ensuring that the legacy of the golden age of athletics lives on.

The Throwing Giants: Shot Put, Discus, Hammer, and Javelin Masters

In the realm of track and field, a group of athletes with sheer power and strength have earned them the title of "Throwing Giants." These masters of shot put, discus, hammer, and javelin have not only shattered records but also redefined the limits of human potential. In this section, we will delve into the lives and achievements of these remarkable individuals who have left an indelible mark on the world of athletics.

The shot put event has been graced by numerous legends, but perhaps none more iconic than Parry O'Brien. This American powerhouse revolutionized the sport with his innovative "O'Brien Glide" technique, which allowed him to generate more power and distance in his throws. O'Brien's dominance in the 1950s and 1960s earned him four Olympic medals, including two golds, and an incredible 116 consecutive victories in the competition.

In the discus event, the name Al Oerter stands tall among the pantheon of greats. This American athlete's incredible consistency and determination saw him win four consecutive Olympic gold medals from 1956 to 1968, a feat that remains unmatched in the event's history. Oerter's ability to rise to the occasion and deliver his best performances on the biggest stage is a testament to his mental fortitude and competitive spirit.

Several exceptional athletes have dominated the hammer throw, but none more so than Yuriy Sedykh. This Soviet legend's incredible technique and power allowed him to set multiple world records and win two Olympic gold medals. Sedykh's rivalry with fellow Soviet athlete Sergey Litvinov pushed both men to new heights, culminating in a thrilling showdown at the 1986 European Championships, where Sedykh unleashed a world record throw of 86.74 meters that still stands today.

The javelin event has seen its fair share of extraordinary talents, but one name that stands out is Jan Železný. This Czech athlete's incredible speed, strength, and precision propelled him to three Olympic gold medals and five world records. However, Železný's 98.48-meter throw in 1996 remains the pinnacle of javelin mastery, a testament to his relentless pursuit of excellence.

These Throwing Giants have etched their names in the annals of track and field history and inspired countless others to push the boundaries of human performance. Their dedication, perseverance, and unwavering commitment to their craft are shining examples for future generations of athletes. As we celebrate their achievements, we also look forward to the emergence of new legends who will continue to elevate the sport and carry on the legacy of these extraordinary individuals.

The Decathlon and Heptathlon: The Ultimate Test of Athleticism

The decathlon and heptathlon are often considered the pinnacle of athletic achievement, as they require competitors to excel in various disciplines. These multi-event competitions showcase the world's most talented athletes' incredible versatility, strength, and endurance. This section will delve into the fascinating world of the decathlon and heptathlon, exploring the legends who have left an indelible mark on these grueling events.

The decathlon, a men's event, consists of ten track and field disciplines, including the 100 meters, long jump, shot put, high jump, 400 meters, 110 meters hurdles, discus, pole vault, javelin, and 1500 meters. The heptathlon, a women's event, comprises seven disciplines: the 100 meters hurdles, high jump, shot put, 200 meters, long jump, javelin, and 800 meters. Athletes earn points based on their performance in each event, with the overall winner determined by the highest cumulative score.

One of the most iconic decathletes in history is the American athlete Jim Thorpe. Competing in the 1912 Stockholm Olympics, Thorpe dominated the decathlon, setting world records in several events and winning the gold medal. Despite facing numerous challenges throughout his life, including racial discrimination and the stripping of his Olympic medals due to a technicality (which were later reinstated), Thorpe's incredible achievements and indomitable spirit have made him a symbol of perseverance and excellence in the world of athletics.

Another legendary decathlete is the British athlete Daley Thompson. A two-time Olympic gold medalist (1980 and 1984), Thompson was known for his fierce competitiveness and extraordinary work ethic. His intense rivalry with West German athlete Jürgen Hingsen pushed both athletes to break world records and elevate the decathlon to new heights. Thompson's charismatic personality and unwavering dedication to his sport have made him a beloved athletic figure.

In the realm of the heptathlon, one name stands above the rest: Jackie Joyner-Kersee. The American athlete is widely regarded as one of the greatest heptathletes of all time, having won three Olympic gold medals, one silver, and two bronze. Joyner-Kersee's incredible range of talents allowed her to excel in every discipline, setting world records in both the heptathlon and the long jump. Her remarkable achievements, tireless advocacy for women's sports, and philanthropic efforts have made Joyner-Kersee an enduring inspiration for athletes worldwide.

The decathlon and heptathlon are the ultimate tests of athleticism, demanding a rare combination of speed, strength, agility, and endurance. The legends of these events, such as Jim Thorpe, Daley Thompson, and Jackie Joyner-Kersee, have left an indelible mark on the track and field world, inspiring countless athletes to push their limits and strive for greatness. As we continue to marvel at the incredible feats of these multi-event masters, we are reminded of the true essence of athleticism: the relentless pursuit of excellence in the face of adversity.

The Trailblazers: Breaking Barriers and Shattering Records

In the annals of sports history, there are those who excel in their respective disciplines and redefine the boundaries of human potential. Through their sheer determination and indomitable spirit, these trailblazers have broken barriers and shattered records, inspiring generations of athletes to follow in their footsteps. In the Golden Age of Athletics, track and field legends emerged as true trailblazers, pushing the limits of what was thought possible and leaving an indelible mark on the world of sports.

One such trailblazer was Jesse Owens, an African-American sprinter who defied the odds and racial prejudice to win four gold medals at the 1936 Berlin Olympics. Owens' victories in the 100 meters, 200 meters, long jump, and 4x100-meter relay not only debunked the myth of Aryan supremacy but also demonstrated the power of sports to unite people across racial and cultural divides.

Another barrier-breaker was Fanny Blankers-Koen, a Dutch athlete who became the first woman to win four gold medals in a single Olympics. Competing in the 1948 London Games, Blankers-Koen triumphed in the 100 meters, 200 meters, 80-meter hurdles, and 4x100-meter relay, earning her the nickname "The Flying Housewife." Her achievements paved the way for greater recognition and opportunities for female athletes in track and field.

The Golden Age of Athletics also witnessed the rise of Emil Zátopek, a Czechoslovak long-distance runner who revolutionized the sport with his unique training methods and relentless work ethic. Zátopek's crowning achievement came at the 1952 Helsinki Olympics, where he won gold in the 5,000 meters, 10,000 meters, and the marathon – a feat that remains unmatched today. His innovative approach to training, which included interval workouts and high-mileage regimens, would later become the foundation for modern long-distance running.

In field events, Al Oerter stands out as a trailblazer who redefined the art of discus throwing. The American athlete won four consecutive Olympic gold medals between 1956 and 1968, setting a new world record with each victory. Oerter's unwavering dedication to his craft and ability to overcome injuries and adversity serve as a testament to the power of perseverance in facing challenges.

The Golden Age of Athletics was also marked by the emergence of multi-event athletes who showcased their versatility and all-around prowess. Rafer Johnson and Jackie Joyner-Kersee stand out as trailblazers in the decathlon and heptathlon, respectively. Johnson's gold medal-winning performance at the 1960 Rome Olympics and Joyner-Kersee's world record-breaking feats in the 1980s and 1990s exemplify the dedication, discipline, and determination required to excel in these grueling tests of athleticism.

These trailblazers and countless others have left an indelible mark on the world of track and field. Their barrier-breaking achievements and record-shattering performances have redefined the limits of human potential and inspired generations of athletes to push themselves to greater heights. So, as we celebrate the Golden Age of Athletics, let us remember and honor the trailblazers who have paved the way for the legends of today and tomorrow.

The Legacy: How Track and Field Legends Inspired Future Generations

The Golden Age of Athletics was a time of unparalleled achievement and groundbreaking performances. The track and field legends of this era left an indelible mark on the history of sports and inspired countless athletes who followed in their footsteps. Their stories of triumph, perseverance, and dedication continue to resonate with future generations, shaping the landscape of athletics and fostering a culture of excellence.

One of the most significant ways these legends have impacted future generations is by breaking barriers and redefining what is possible in human performance. For example, athletes like Jesse Owens, who defied racial prejudice and emerged as a symbol of hope and unity during the 1936 Berlin Olympics, showed the world that talent and determination can overcome even the most daunting obstacles. Similarly, Fanny Blankers-Koen, the "Flying Housewife," challenged gender stereotypes and proved that women could excel in multiple disciplines, paving the way for female athletes to pursue their dreams without limitations.

The track and field legends of the Golden Age also inspired future generations through their relentless pursuit of excellence. Athletes like Paavo Nurmi, the "Flying Finn," who dominated distance running in the 1920s, and Emil Zátopek, the "Czech Locomotive," who revolutionized training methods and won an unprecedented triple gold at the 1952 Helsinki Olympics, set new standards for what could be achieved in their respective events. Their unwavering commitment to pushing the boundaries of human potential has motivated countless athletes to strive for greatness and surpass their limits.

Moreover, the sportsmanship and camaraderie displayed by these legends have served as a model for future generations. The iconic image of Derek Redmond, supported by his father, as he hobbled across the finish line in the 1992 Barcelona Olympics, exemplifies the spirit of resilience and determination that defines the essence of track and field. Similarly, the friendship and mutual respect between Carl Lewis and Mike Powell, who pushed each other to new heights in the long jump, demonstrate the power of healthy competition and the importance of supporting one's peers.

The impact of the Golden Age of Athletics extends beyond sports, as the lessons learned from these track and field legends have permeated various aspects of society. Their stories of overcoming adversity, breaking barriers, and striving for excellence have inspired countless individuals to pursue their passions and make a difference in their own lives and the lives of others. In addition, the values of hard work, discipline, and perseverance, embodied by these legends, have become cornerstones of personal growth and success in various fields.

In conclusion, the track and field legends of the Golden Age of Athletics have left an enduring legacy that inspires future generations. Their groundbreaking achievements, unwavering commitment to excellence, and indomitable spirit have shaped the landscape of athletics and transcended the boundaries of sports, influencing countless lives and fostering a culture of resilience, determination, and success. As we celebrate their remarkable accomplishments, we are reminded of the power of the human spirit and the limitless potential within each of us.

The Enduring Impact of the Golden Age of Athletics

As we conclude our journey through the Golden Age of Athletics, it is essential to reflect on the enduring impact these track and field legends have had on the world of sports and beyond. Their remarkable achievements, unwavering dedication, and relentless pursuit of excellence have inspired countless athletes and left an indelible mark on the history of human endeavor.

The Golden Age of Athletics was when the world witnessed the true potential of human physicality and the power of the human spirit. These track and field legends pushed the boundaries of what was thought possible, breaking records and setting new standards for future generations to aspire to. Their accomplishments have become the benchmarks against which all athletes are measured, and their stories continue to captivate and inspire.

The impact of these legends extends far beyond the realm of athletics. They have become symbols of perseverance, determination, and the pursuit of greatness. Their stories have taught us that anything is possible with hard work, dedication, and an unwavering belief in oneself. They have shown us that barriers can be broken and that the human spirit can overcome even the most daunting challenges.

Moreover, the trailblazers of the Golden Age of Athletics have played a crucial role in breaking down societal barriers and promoting inclusivity in sports. They have paved the way for athletes of all backgrounds, genders, and abilities to compete on the world stage, proving that greatness is not limited by race, gender, or physical limitations. In addition, their courage and resilience have inspired countless individuals to challenge stereotypes and pursue their dreams, regardless of the obstacles they may face.

The Golden Age of Athletics legacy is found in more than just the record books or the annals of sports history. It is alive in the hearts and minds of every athlete who steps onto the track, field, or court, striving to push their limits and achieve their personal best. It is present in the coaches, trainers, and mentors who dedicate their lives to nurturing the next generation of sports legends. And it is evident in the millions of fans who continue to celebrate and honor the achievements of these extraordinary individuals.

In conclusion, the Golden Age of Athletics has impacted the world of sports and the human spirit. This era's track and field legends have shown us the true potential of human physicality, the power of determination, and the importance of breaking barriers. Their stories continue to inspire and captivate, reminding us that greatness is not a destination but a journey that requires perseverance, dedication, and an unwavering belief in oneself. As we look to the future, let us carry the lessons and legacy of the Golden Age of Athletics with us and continue striving for excellence in all we do.

3

THE BEAUTIFUL GAME: SOCCER LEGENDS

Soccer, the Beautiful Game

Soccer, or football as it is known in most parts of the world, is a sport that transcends borders, languages, and cultures. With over four billion fans across the globe, it is undeniably the world's most popular sport. The beautiful game, as it is often called, has a rich history filled with iconic moments, unforgettable matches, and legendary players who have left an indelible mark on the sport. In this chapter, we will delve into the lives and careers of some of the most exceptional soccer legends who have graced the pitch and captivated the hearts of millions.

The beauty of soccer lies in its simplicity. All that is needed is a ball, a field, and a group of players eager to showcase their skills and passion for the game. This simplicity has allowed soccer to flourish in every corner of the world, from the favelas of Brazil to the streets of London and from the dusty fields of Africa to the manicured pitches of Europe's elite clubs. The sport's universal appeal has given rise to diverse talents, each with unique style, flair, and impact on the game.

In this chapter, we will explore the stories of soccer legends from various positions on the field, as well as the masterminds who orchestrated their success from the sidelines. We will begin by paying homage to the pioneers who laid the groundwork for the modern game and set the stage for future soccer stars. From there, we will delve into the lives and careers of legendary goalkeepers, defenders, midfielders, and strikers, highlighting their most memorable moments and the qualities that set them apart from their peers.

As we journey through the annals of soccer history, we will also examine the rivalries and partnerships that have shaped the careers of these legends, as well as their unforgettable performances on the world stage in international tournaments. Furthermore, we will celebrate the trailblazers who broke barriers and transcended the sport, using their platform to inspire change and make a lasting impact beyond the confines of the soccer pitch.

Finally, we will look to the future, identifying the rising stars and the next generation of soccer legends poised to carry the torch and continue the rich legacy of the beautiful game. Through their stories, we will gain a deeper appreciation for the dedication, talent, and passion that have made soccer the world's most beloved sport and its icons the stuff of legend.

So, lace up your boots, grab a ball, and join us as we embark on this journey through the annals of soccer history, celebrating the legends who have left an indelible mark on the beautiful game and inspired generations of fans and players alike.

The Pioneers: Early Soccer Legends Who Shaped the Game

Soccer, or football as it is known in many parts of the world, has a rich and storied history that dates back over a century. The sport has evolved significantly since its inception, and much of this progress can be attributed to the pioneering players who helped shape the game into what it is today. These early soccer legends displayed exceptional skill and talent on the field and contributed to the sport's development through their innovative tactics, techniques, and sportsmanship. This section will explore the lives and careers of some of the most influential pioneers in soccer history.

One of the earliest soccer legends is Arthur Wharton, widely regarded as the world's first black professional footballer. Born in Ghana in 1865, Wharton moved to England in the 1880s and quickly made a name for himself with his incredible athleticism and goal-keeping prowess. Despite facing racial discrimination, Wharton broke barriers and paved the way for future generations of black players in the sport.

Another game pioneer was Billy Meredith, a Welsh winger who played for Manchester City and Manchester United in the early 20th century. Meredith was known for his exceptional dribbling skills and ability to score goals, making him one of the first true superstars of the sport. He was also a key figure in forming the Players' Union, which sought to improve professional footballers' working conditions and rights.

In tactics and strategy, few names stand out more than Herbert Chapman. As a manager, Chapman revolutionized the game with his innovative ideas and formations, most notably the "WM" formation, which laid the groundwork for modern soccer tactics. Under his guidance, both Huddersfield Town and Arsenal enjoyed immense success, with Chapman's teams winning numerous league titles and FA Cups.

No discussion of soccer pioneers would be complete without mentioning the legendary Pelé. Born in Brazil in 1940, Pelé burst onto the international scene at 17, scoring a hat-trick in the 1958 World Cup semifinal and helping Brazil secure their first-ever World Cup title. Throughout his illustrious career, Pelé scored over 1,000 professional goals and won three World Cups, cementing his status as one of the greatest players ever. His skill, flair, and sportsmanship captivated audiences worldwide and inspired countless young players to take up the sport.

These early soccer legends dazzled fans with their incredible abilities on the field and played a crucial role in shaping the game we know and love today. Their innovation, determination, and passion for the sport laid the foundation for future generations of players. In addition, they ensured that soccer would continue to captivate and inspire fans around the globe. As we delve deeper into the world of soccer legends, it is essential to remember and celebrate the pioneers who blazed the trail for those who followed in their footsteps.

Goalkeepers: The Last Line of Defense and Their Unforgettable Saves

In the beautiful game of soccer, goalkeepers hold a unique and vital position. As the last line of defense, they are entrusted with preventing the opposing team from scoring. Often referred to as the "guardians of the goal," these players possess a combination of physical prowess, mental fortitude, and technical skills that set them apart from their teammates. In this section, we will delve into the world of goalkeeping legends, exploring their incredible saves and their impact on the sport.

One cannot discuss goalkeeping legends without mentioning Lev Yashin, the "Black Spider." Hailing from the Soviet Union, Yashin is considered the greatest goalkeeper ever. With his exceptional reflexes, agility, and shot-stopping ability, he revolutionized the position and set the standard for future generations. Yashin's most memorable save came in the 1966 World Cup when he denied Hungarian striker Ferenc Bene with a tremendous one-handed stop, helping the Soviet Union secure a 2-1 victory.

Another iconic figure in the world of goalkeeping is Italy's Dino Zoff. Known for his calm demeanor and outstanding positioning, Zoff captained Italy to World Cup glory in 1982 at the age of 40, making him the oldest player to win the prestigious tournament. His most unforgettable save came in the 1982 World Cup semifinal against Poland, when he expertly parried a powerful shot from point-blank range, ensuring Italy's progression to the final.

Gianluigi Buffon, another Italian legend, has enjoyed a remarkable career spanning over two decades. With his commanding presence, exceptional reflexes, and ability to read the game, Buffon has earned his place among the all-time greats. One of his most iconic saves occurred in the 2006 World Cup semifinal against Germany when he miraculously tipped a thunderous shot from Lukas Podolski over the crossbar, helping Italy advance to the final and ultimately win the tournament.

The list of goalkeeping legends would only be complete by mentioning the likes of Peter Schmeichel, Oliver Kahn, and Iker Casillas. Schmeichel, known as the "Great Dane," was a key figure in Manchester United's dominance during the 1990s, while Kahn's intimidating presence and fierce competitiveness earned him the nickname "Der Titan." On the other hand, Casillas was the embodiment of grace under pressure, leading Spain to their first-ever World Cup victory in 2010.

These goalkeeping legends have not only made countless unforgettable saves but have also inspired generations of aspiring goalkeepers. Their fearlessness, dedication, and unwavering commitment to their teams have left an indelible mark on the beautiful game. As we continue to marvel at their incredible feats, we are reminded of the crucial role that goalkeepers play in soccer and the immense pressure they face every time they step onto the pitch.

Defenders: The Art of Stopping Goals and Building Attacks

In the beautiful game of soccer, the spotlight often shines on the goalscorers and playmakers. However, the unsung heroes of the sport are the defenders, whose primary responsibility is to prevent the opposition from scoring. These players possess a unique blend of physicality, intelligence, and technical skill, which allows them to excel in their roles. In this section, we will explore the art of defending and celebrating some of soccer's greatest defenders.

Defending in soccer is a multifaceted discipline that requires a deep understanding of the game. A great defender must possess excellent positioning, anticipation, and decision-making skills to read the game and react accordingly. They must also be vital in one-on-one situations, winning tackles and aerial duels to regain possession for their team. Moreover, defenders play a crucial role in building attacks from the back with their accurate passing and composure on the ball.

Franz Beckenbauer was one of the earliest and most influential defenders in soccer history. Nicknamed "Der Kaiser," the German legend revolutionized the sweeper role, a position that allowed him to roam freely behind the backline and initiate attacks with his exceptional vision and passing range. Beckenbauer's elegant style of play and tactical intelligence set the standard for future defenders.

Another iconic defending figure is Franco Baresi, the Italian maestro who spent his entire career at AC Milan. Baresi was renowned for his incredible reading of the game, which enabled him to make countless interceptions and well-timed tackles. In addition, his leadership and organizational skills were instrumental in forming one of the most formidable backlines in soccer history alongside fellow legend Paolo Maldini.

Maldini, a versatile defender who could play as a center-back or left-back, epitomized elegance, and composure on the field. His ability to nullify the threat of even the most skillful attackers earned him a reputation as one of the greatest defenders of all time. Maldini's longevity and consistency at the highest level, combined with his numerous domestic and international titles, make him a true soccer legend.

In recent times, defenders such as Sergio Ramos, Virgil van Dijk, and Gerard Piqué have continued redefining the art of defending. These players excel in their defensive duties and contribute significantly to their team's attacking play with their precise passing and aerial prowess from set pieces.

The role of the defender in soccer has evolved over the years, with modern defenders expected to be more than just a physical presence at the back. Today's defenders must be tactically astute, technically proficient, and comfortable on the ball, as they play a crucial role in stopping goals and building attacks.

In conclusion, the art of defending in soccer is a complex and often underappreciated aspect. However, the legends mentioned in this section and countless others have left an indelible mark on the sport with their defensive prowess and ability to contribute to their team's attacking play. As the beautiful game continues to evolve, we can look forward to witnessing the rise of even more exceptional defenders who will carry on the legacy of these soccer legends.

Midfield Maestros: The Playmakers Who Controlled the Game

In the heart of every great soccer team lies a midfield maestro, a player with the unique ability to control the game's tempo, dictate play, and create opportunities for their teammates. These playmakers are the architects of the beautiful game, weaving intricate patterns on the field and orchestrating the movements of their fellow players. In this section, we will delve into the careers of some of the most influential midfield maestros in soccer history, exploring their styles, memorable moments, and lasting impact on the sport.

One cannot discuss midfield maestros without mentioning the

legendary Pelé. Hailing from Brazil, Pelé is often regarded as the greatest soccer player of all time. With his exceptional vision, precise passing, and unparalleled dribbling skills, Pelé was the epitome of a midfield maestro. His ability to create goal-scoring opportunities for himself and his teammates was unmatched, leading Brazil to three FIFA World Cup titles in 1958, 1962, and 1970.

Another iconic playmaker is Diego Maradona, the Argentine genius who dazzled fans with his extraordinary dribbling skills, creativity, and vision. Maradona's most famous moment came in the 1986 World Cup. He single-handedly led Argentina to victory, scoring the infamous "Hand of God" goal and the "Goal of the Century" against England in the quarterfinals. His ability to control the game and create magic on the field earned him a place among the all-time greats.

From the Netherlands, Johan Cruyff was a midfield maestro who revolutionized the game with his unique style of play, known as "Total Football." Cruyff's intelligence, vision, and technical skills allowed him to excel in multiple positions on the field, making him a versatile and invaluable asset to his team. Cruyff's influence on soccer is still felt today as a player and later as a manager, with many modern tactics and philosophies rooted in his innovative approach to the game.

Spanish midfielders Xavi and Andrés Iniesta have recently been the epitome of midfield maestros. Playing for FC Barcelona and the Spanish national team, the duo formed a formidable partnership, dominating the midfield with their exceptional passing, vision, and understanding of the game. Together, they led Spain to their first-ever World Cup title in 2010 and helped Barcelona achieve numerous domestic and international titles, including four UEFA Champions League trophies.

The list of midfield maestros is extensive, with each player bringing their unique flair and style to the beautiful game. From the elegance of Frenchman Zinedine Zidane to the tenacity of Englishman Steven Gerrard, these playmakers have left an indelible mark on soccer history. Their ability to control the game, create opportunities, and inspire their teammates has made them legends of the sport, and their influence will continue to shape the future of soccer for generations to come.

Strikers: The Goal-Scoring Machines and Their Legendary Moments

In the beautiful game of soccer, strikers are often the most celebrated and revered players on the pitch. These goal-scoring machines possess an uncanny ability to find the back of the net, often in the most crucial moments of a match. As a result, their legendary exploits have been etched into the annals of soccer history, inspiring generations of fans and aspiring players alike. In this section, we will delve into the careers of some of the most prolific and iconic strikers in the sport's history, reliving their unforgettable moments and exploring the qualities that set them apart.

One cannot discuss soccer legends without mentioning the Brazilian phenomenon, Pelé. Widely regarded as one of the greatest players, Pelé's incredible goal-scoring prowess saw him net over 1,000 career goals, a record that still stands today. His extraordinary skill, agility, and creativity on the field led Brazil to three FIFA World Cup titles in 1958, 1962, and 1970. Among his many legendary moments, his audacious dummy against Uruguay in the 1970 World Cup, which left the goalkeeper floundering, remains one of the most iconic plays in soccer history.

Another striker who left an indelible mark on the sport is Argentina's, Diego Maradona. Blessed with incredible dribbling skills, vision, and a lethal left foot, Maradona's career was filled with magical moments. His infamous "Hand of God" goal and his mesmerizing solo run against England in the 1986 World Cup quarterfinals, where he dribbled past five players to score, are still talked about today. Maradona's ability to single-handedly change the course of a game made him one of the most feared and respected strikers in soccer history.

The modern era of soccer has also seen its fair share of goal-scoring legends. Cristiano Ronaldo and Lionel Messi, two of the greatest players of their generation, have consistently shattered records and thrilled fans with their incredible goal-scoring exploits. Ronaldo's remarkable athleticism, powerful shots, and aerial prowess have seen him score over 700 career goals. At the same time, Messi's sublime dribbling, vision, and precise finishing have earned him the title of the sport's all-time top scorer in a single European club competition.

Other notable strikers who have left their mark on the sport include Thierry Henry, whose elegance, speed, and clinical finishing made him one of the most feared forwards in the world; Ronaldo Nazário, the Brazilian phenomenon whose explosive pace and skillful dribbling earned him the nickname "The Phenomenon"; and Gerd Müller, the German goal machine whose predatory instincts and remarkable scoring ability saw him net an astonishing 68 goals in just 62 international appearances.

These legendary strikers have provided fans with countless unforgettable moments and shaped the way the game is played today. Their unique styles, techniques, and abilities have influenced generations of players, and their names will forever be synonymous with the art of goal-scoring. As we look to the future, we eagerly await the emergence of new striking talents who will continue to push the boundaries of what is possible on the soccer field and etch their names alongside these iconic legends.

The Managers: Masterminds Behind the Success of Soccer Legends

In the beautiful game of soccer, the spotlight often shines on the players who dazzle us with their skills, goals, and memorable moments. However, behind every successful team and legendary player, a mastermind orchestrates the symphony of talent on the field. These are the managers, the tacticians, and the visionaries who have shaped the careers of soccer legends and guided their teams to glory.

The role of a manager in soccer is multifaceted, encompassing not only tactical acumen but also man-management, motivation, and adaptability. A great manager can inspire his players to reach new heights, instill a winning mentality, and create a cohesive unit that functions as a single entity on the field. In this section, we will explore the careers and contributions of some of soccer's most influential and successful managers.

One cannot discuss soccer managers without mentioning Sir Alex Ferguson, the legendary Scottish manager who led Manchester United to an unprecedented era of success. Under his guidance, the Red Devils won 13 Premier League titles, 5 FA Cups, and 2 UEFA Champions League trophies. Sir Alex was renowned for his ability to nurture young talents, such as the famous "Class of '92," which included soccer icons like David Beckham, Ryan Giggs, and Paul Scholes. His man-management skills, tactical nous, and never-say-die attitude made him one of the sport's most respected and feared managers.

Another iconic figure in soccer management is the late Johan Cruyff, who revolutionized the game as a player and coach. As the manager of Barcelona, Cruyff implemented his philosophy of "Total Football," which emphasized fluidity, positional interchange, and attacking flair. This approach laid the foundation for the modern Barcelona style. It influenced a generation of managers, including Pep Guardiola, who would become a legend in his own right.

Guardiola, a disciple of Cruyff, has enjoyed immense success as a manager, winning numerous domestic and international titles with Barcelona, Bayern Munich, and Manchester City. His tactical innovations, such as the "false nine" and "inverted fullbacks," have made him one of the most influential coaches in recent history. Guardiola's ability to adapt his tactics to different leagues and squads while maintaining his core principles has solidified his status as a managerial great.

The world of soccer has also seen its fair share of charismatic and enigmatic managers, such as José Mourinho and Jürgen Klopp. Mourinho, known as "The Special One," has achieved success with multiple clubs, including Porto, Chelsea, Inter Milan, and Real Madrid. His pragmatic and often controversial approach has earned him admirers and critics, but his impressive trophy haul speaks for itself. On the other hand, Klopp's infectious enthusiasm and "heavy metal football" philosophy have endeared him to fans and players alike, as he has transformed Borussia Dortmund and Liverpool into European powerhouses.

In conclusion, the managers highlighted in this section have played a crucial role in shaping the careers of soccer legends and the sport itself. Their tactical innovations, man-management skills, and ability to inspire their teams have left an indelible mark on soccer history. As the beautiful game continues to evolve, we can look forward to witnessing the rise of new managerial masterminds who will guide the next generation of soccer legends to glory.

Rivalries and Partnerships: The Duels and Bonds That Defined Careers

In soccer, rivalries and partnerships have played a significant role in shaping the careers of legends. These intense duels and unbreakable bonds have not only defined the players' careers but have also captivated fans and created unforgettable moments in the sport's history. This section will delve into some of the most iconic rivalries and partnerships that have left an indelible mark on the beautiful game.

One of the most famous rivalries in soccer history is the one between Argentine legend Diego Maradona and Brazilian icon Pelé. Both players are considered the greatest of all time, and their on-field battles and off-field debates about who was the better player have fueled the fire of this rivalry for decades. Their contrasting styles of play, with Maradona's dribbling wizardry and Pelé's goal-scoring prowess, have made their duels a fascinating spectacle for soccer enthusiasts.

Another iconic rivalry is between Cristiano Ronaldo and Lionel Messi, two of the most dominant players in the modern era. Their brilliance and relentless pursuit of greatness have seen them break numerous records and win countless titles. The rivalry between these two legends has transcended club football, with fans and pundits often comparing their achievements and debating who is the superior player.

While rivalries often take center stage, partnerships in soccer have also played a crucial role in defining careers. For example, the telepathic understanding between Xavi Hernandez and Andres Iniesta, two of the greatest midfielders in history, was the backbone of the dominant Barcelona and Spanish national teams. Their ability to control the game's tempo and create goal-scoring opportunities for their teammates was a joy to watch and a nightmare for opponents.

Another legendary partnership was between Thierry Henry and Dennis Bergkamp at Arsenal. The Frenchman's speed and finishing ability, combined with the Dutchman's vision and technique, made them one of the most feared attacking duos in the history of the English Premier League. Their understanding of the field was instrumental in Arsenal's success during the early 2000s, including their unbeaten league campaign in the 2003-2004 season.

Rivalries and partnerships in soccer have not only defined the careers of legends but have also shaped the narrative of the sport. These intense duels and unbreakable bonds have provided fans with countless unforgettable moments and contributed to the beautiful game's rich history. As soccer continues to evolve, new rivalries and partnerships will emerge, further enriching the legacy of the sport and its legends.

The World Stage: Unforgettable Performances in International Tournaments

As the world's most popular sport, soccer has always been a stage for the most extraordinary talents to showcase their skills and etch their names in history. International tournaments, such as the FIFA World Cup and the UEFA European Championship, have provided the perfect platform for soccer legends to shine and leave an indelible mark on the hearts and minds of fans across the globe. In this section, we will revisit some of the most unforgettable performances by soccer legends in international tournaments.

One cannot discuss soccer legends without mentioning the name Pelé. The Brazilian icon, often regarded as the greatest soccer player of all time, burst onto the international scene at 17 during the 1958 World Cup in Sweden. Pelé scored a hat-trick in the semifinal against France and followed it up with a brace against the host nation in the final, helping Brazil secure their first World Cup title. His skill, flair, and goal-scoring prowess would lead Brazil to two more World Cup triumphs in 1962 and 1970, cementing his status as a true soccer legend.

Another iconic figure in the world of soccer is Argentina's Diego Maradona. His performance in the 1986 World Cup in Mexico is the stuff of legends. Maradona single-handedly guided Argentina to their second World Cup title, scoring five goals and providing five assists. His infamous "Hand of God" goal and his mesmerizing solo run against England in the quarterfinals, where he dribbled past five players to score what would later be known as the "Goal of the Century," are still etched in the memories of soccer fans worldwide.

The 1998 World Cup in France saw the rise of another soccer legend, Zinedine Zidane. The French maestro was pivotal in guiding the host nation to their first-ever World Cup title. Zidane's elegance, vision, and technique were displayed throughout the tournament, culminating in a brace in the final against Brazil. His two headers in the first half set the tone for a dominant French victory, and Zidane's status as a soccer icon was firmly established.

More recently, the 2014 World Cup in Brazil witnessed the heroics of Germany's Miroslav Klose. The prolific striker broke the all-time World Cup goal-scoring record, previously held by Brazil's Ronaldo, by netting his 16th goal in the tournament. Klose's remarkable feat was instrumental in Germany's journey to their fourth World Cup title, and his name will forever be synonymous with goal-scoring excellence on the world stage.

These unforgettable performances in international tournaments are just a few examples of the countless moments that have shaped the careers of soccer legends. The passion, skill, and determination displayed by these icons have brought glory to their respective nations and inspired generations of soccer fans and aspiring players. As we continue to witness the beautiful game unfold on the world stage, there is no doubt that new legends will emerge, and their stories will be etched in the annals of soccer history.

Breaking Barriers: Soccer Legends Who Transcended the Sport

Soccer, as a sport, has always had the power to unite people from different backgrounds, cultures, and nations. However, some soccer legends have gone beyond the boundaries of the sport, breaking barriers and transcending the game in ways that have left an indelible mark on society. In this section, we will explore the stories of these extraordinary individuals who have used their talent, influence, and passion for soccer to make a difference in the world.

One of the most iconic figures in soccer history, Pelé, is known for his incredible skills on the field and his role as a global ambassador for the sport. Hailing from Brazil, Pelé's rise to fame in the 1950s and 1960s coincided with significant social and political change in his home country. As a black player who achieved international success, Pelé broke racial barriers and inspired millions of people worldwide. His commitment to social causes, such as education and poverty alleviation, has further cemented his status as a transcendent figure in soccer.

Another soccer legend transcending the sport is the enigmatic Frenchman Zinedine Zidane. Born to Algerian immigrants in Marseille, Zidane's journey to becoming one of the greatest players is a testament to the power of hard work, determination, and resilience. Throughout his career, Zidane has used his platform to speak out against racism and promote tolerance and understanding between different cultures. His efforts to bridge the divide between Europe and the Arab world have earned him widespread admiration and respect, both on and off the field.

The story of Didier Drogba, the Ivorian striker who played for Chelsea, is another example of a soccer legend who has transcended the sport. In 2006, following a brutal civil war in his home country, Drogba used his influence to bring about a ceasefire and promote peace and reconciliation in Ivory Coast. His humanitarian work, which includes establishing the Didier Drogba Foundation, has focused on providing healthcare, education, and other essential services to vulnerable African communities.

The impact of these soccer legends extends beyond their incredible achievements on the field. They have used their fame and influence to break down barriers, challenge stereotypes, and inspire positive change. Their stories serve as a reminder that soccer is more than just a game; it is a powerful force that can unite people, bridge divides, and transform lives. As we look to the future, we can only hope that the next generation of soccer legends will continue to carry this torch and use their talents to improve the world.

The Future: Rising Stars and the Next Generation of Soccer Legends

As we celebrate the incredible achievements of soccer's greatest legends, we must look forward and recognize the rising stars who are poised to carry the torch and continue the sport's rich legacy. The future of soccer is bright, with a new generation of talented players emerging from all corners of the globe, eager to etch their names in the annals of history. In this section, we will explore some of the most promising young talents who have the potential to become the next soccer legends.

One of the most exciting prospects in world soccer is Kylian Mbappé, a French forward who has significantly impacted club and international levels. Bursting onto the scene as a teenager, Mbappé's incredible speed, skill, and goal-scoring ability have drawn comparisons to legends such as Thierry Henry and Pelé. With a World Cup title under his belt at just 19 years old, the sky is the limit for this young superstar.

Another player who has captured the imagination of soccer fans worldwide is Erling Haaland, a Norwegian striker with a seemingly insatiable appetite for goals. Haaland's combination of size, strength, and finishing ability has made him one of the most feared forwards in the game today. As he continues to develop and refine his skills, there is no doubt that Haaland has the potential to become one of the all-time greats.

In the midfield, English sensation Phil Foden has emerged as a creative force for Manchester City and the national team. Often compared to his compatriot and fellow legend Paul Gascoigne, Foden's vision, passing, and dribbling skills have made him a standout performer in a highly competitive environment. As he continues to mature and gain experience, Foden is well on his way to becoming a soccer legend in his own right.

On the defensive side of the game, Dutch center-back Matthijs de Ligt has already established himself as one of the world's best at a young age. With intelligence, physicality, and technical ability, de Ligt has all the tools necessary to become a dominant force in the sport for years.

Of course, these are just a few examples of the many talented young players set to take the soccer world by storm. As the sport continues to evolve and grow, there is no doubt that we will witness the rise of even more extraordinary talents who will redefine what it means to be a soccer legend.

In conclusion, the future of soccer is in excellent hands, with a new generation of stars ready to carry on the legacy of the legends who came before them. As fans of the beautiful game, we can look forward to witnessing the incredible feats and unforgettable moments that these rising stars will undoubtedly provide. The next chapter in soccer's storied history is just beginning, and we can't wait to see what these future legends have in store for us.

The Enduring Legacy of Soccer's Greatest Legends

As we reach the end of our journey through the world of soccer legends, it is essential to reflect on these extraordinary individuals' impact on the sport and the world at large. From the pioneers who laid the groundwork for modern soccer to the rising stars who promise to carry the torch into the future, these legends have left an indelible mark on the beautiful game.

The stories of these soccer legends are not just about their incredible skills, record-breaking achievements, and unforgettable moments on the field. They are also about the passion, dedication, and resilience that drove them to overcome obstacles and reach the pinnacle of their sport. These qualities have inspired millions of fans and aspiring players worldwide, fostering a love for the game that transcends borders, languages, and cultures.

The legacy of these soccer legends is evident in the countless records they have set, the trophies they have won, and the way they have shaped the game's evolution. Their innovative tactics, techniques, and styles of play have influenced generations of players and coaches, pushing the boundaries of what is possible on the field. As a result, soccer has become a more dynamic, exciting, and entertaining sport for fans to enjoy.

Moreover, the rivalries and partnerships between these legends have added another layer of intrigue and drama to the game. These intense duels and close bonds have not only fueled the players' competitive spirit but also captivated the imagination of fans, creating unforgettable memories that will be cherished for years to come.

Soccer legends have also played a crucial role in breaking down barriers and promoting social change. By challenging stereotypes, fighting for equality, and using their platforms to raise awareness about important issues, these icons have transcended the sport and become role models for people from all walks of life.

As we look to the future, it is clear that the next generation of soccer legends has some big shoes to fill. However, the passion, talent, and ambition these rising stars display give us every reason to believe that they will continue elevating the game to new heights. As they write their chapters in the annals of soccer history, they will undoubtedly draw inspiration from the legends who came before them, ensuring that the beautiful game remains a source of joy, excitement, and inspiration for future generations.

In conclusion, the enduring legacy of soccer's greatest legends is a testament to the power of the beautiful game to captivate our hearts and minds. So, as we celebrate their remarkable achievements and remember their unforgettable moments, let us also appreciate their profound impact on the sport and the world beyond. Through their passion, skill, and determination, soccer has become the world's most popular sport, uniting people from all corners of the globe in their love for the beautiful game.

4
THE COURT KINGS: BASKETBALL LEGENDS

Surreal Basketball Moment

Basketball, a sport that has captivated the hearts and minds of millions across the globe, is a game that has evolved tremendously since its inception in 1891. From the humble beginnings of a peach basket and a soccer ball to the high-flying, fast-paced spectacle that it is today, basketball has produced some of the most iconic and influential athletes in sports history. These legends, known as the Court Kings, have left an indelible mark on the game and have transcended the sport, becoming cultural icons and inspiring generations of fans and players alike.

The Court Kings are a diverse group of individuals who have each brought their unique skills, talents, and personalities to the hardwood. They have dazzled us with their athleticism, awed us with their precision, and inspired us with their determination and passion for the game. These legends have broken records, shattered barriers, and set new standards for excellence on and off the court.

In this chapter, we will delve into the lives and careers of these game changers, exploring their impact on the sport of basketball and the world at large. We will journey through the sport's early days, highlighting the pioneers who founded the game we know and love today. We will marvel at the high-flying dunkers who have defied gravity and redefined the limits of human athleticism. We will celebrate the playmakers, the floor generals who have orchestrated some of the most memorable moments in basketball history. We will pay homage to the sharpshooters, the marksmen who have displayed unparalleled accuracy from beyond the arc. We will honor the big men, the towering giants who have dominated the paint and altered the course of games with their sheer presence. We will recognize the two-way stars, the versatile players who have excelled on both ends of the court, showcasing their offensive and defensive prowess. We will also acknowledge the international icons who have expanded the game's reach and popularity across the globe.

In addition, we will pay tribute to the masterminds behind the success of these legends – the coaches who have guided, mentored, and shaped the careers of these extraordinary athletes. Next, we will delve into the impressive achievements and milestones that have etched the names of these Court Kings into the annals of basketball history. Finally, we will explore the legacy of these legends, examining how their impact on the game continues to inspire and influence future generations of basketball players and fans.

Join us as we embark on this journey through the lives and careers of the Court Kings, the game-changers who have forever altered the landscape of basketball and left an enduring impact on the hearts and minds of those who have witnessed their greatness.

The Pioneers: Early Legends Who Shaped the Sport

As we know it today, basketball is a fast-paced, high-scoring, and exhilarating sport that has captured the hearts of millions of fans worldwide. However, the game we love is the same as the contributions of its early pioneers. These trailblazing legends set the foundation for modern basketball and paved the way for future players to excel and innovate. In this section, we will delve into the lives and careers of some of the most influential pioneers who shaped the sport and left an indelible mark on the history of basketball.

One can only discuss the early legends of basketball by mentioning the man who started it all, Dr. James Naismith. In 1891, Naismith, a Canadian physical education instructor, invented the game to keep his students active during winter. With 13 basic rules, a soccer ball, and two peach baskets, Naismith created a sport that would eventually become a global phenomenon. Although Naismith never played the game professionally, his invention laid the groundwork for the sport's future success.

Another pioneer who significantly impacted the development of basketball was George Mikan. Standing at 6'10", Mikan was one of the first dominant big men in the sport. His size and skill set revolutionized the center position, forcing the league to implement new rules, such as goaltending and widening the key, to counter his dominance. Mikan's success in the 1940s and 1950s with the Minneapolis Lakers paved the way for future big men like Bill Russell, Wilt Chamberlain, and Kareem Abdul-Jabbar.

Bill Russell's impact on the sport cannot be overstated. As a member of the Boston Celtics in the 1950s and 1960s, Russell was a defensive force, winning an astounding 11 NBA championships in his 13-year career. His shot-blocking and rebounding prowess set the standard for defensive excellence in the league. Russell's rivalry with Wilt Chamberlain, another early legend, captivated fans and helped popularize the sport during its formative years.

Bob Cousy, known as "The Houdini of the Hardwood," was another pioneer who impacted the game. As a point guard for the Boston Celtics, Cousy's flashy ball-handling skills and exceptional court vision revolutionized the position. In addition, his ability to create scoring opportunities for his teammates through dazzling passes and clever playmaking set the stage for future point guards like Magic Johnson, John Stockton, and Steve Nash.

Finally, we must acknowledge the contributions of the Harlem Globetrotters, an exhibition team founded in 1926 by Abe Saperstein. The Globetrotters were known for their incredible athleticism, showmanship, and comedic antics on the court. They played a crucial role in breaking down racial barriers in the sport and popularizing basketball worldwide. Legends like Meadowlark Lemon, Marques Haynes, and Goose Tatum entertained fans while showcasing their exceptional skills, inspiring countless young players to take up the sport.

In conclusion, the pioneers of basketball were instrumental in shaping the sport into what it is today. Their innovations, skills, and passion for the game laid the foundation for future players to build upon. These early legends set the stage for the modern game and left a lasting legacy that inspires and captivates basketball fans worldwide.

High-Flying Dunkers: The Aerial Artists of Basketball

Basketball is a sport that captivates audiences with its fast-paced action, skillful plays, and gravity-defying feats. Among the most thrilling aspects of the game are the high-flying dunkers, who have elevated the sport to new heights with their aerial artistry. These athletes possess a unique combination of athleticism, creativity, and fearlessness, which allows them to soar above the rim and electrify fans with their jaw-dropping dunks. This section will pay homage to the greatest high-flyers in basketball history, whose acrobatic exploits have left an indelible mark on the sport.

The art of dunking can be traced back to the early days of basketball, but it was not until the 1970s and 1980s that the slam dunk became a spectacle. Pioneers like Julius "Dr. J" Erving and David "Skywalker" Thompson dazzled fans with their aerial exploits, paving the way for future generations of high-flyers. Dr. J's iconic free-throw line dunk in the 1976 ABA Slam Dunk Contest remains one of the most memorable moments in basketball history, showcasing the limitless potential of the dunk as a form of artistic expression.

In the 1980s and 1990s, the torch was passed to a new generation of high-flyers, led by the incomparable Michael Jordan. His Airness took the art of dunking to new heights with gravity-defying leaps and acrobatic finishes. Jordan's battles with Dominique, "The Human Highlight Film" Wilkins in the Slam Dunk Contest, are the stuff of legend, as both players pushed the boundaries of what was thought possible on the court. Other notable dunkers from this era include Clyde "The Glide" Drexler, Shawn "Reign Man" Kemp, and Vince "Vinsanity" Carter, who each brought their unique flair to the art of the slam dunk.

The 21st century has seen the continued evolution of the high-flying dunker, with players like LeBron James, Blake Griffin, and Zach LaVine carrying on the tradition of aerial artistry. These modern-day court kings have taken the dunk to new levels of creativity and athleticism, incorporating complex spins, alley-oops, and props into their high-flying exploits. The Slam Dunk Contest has continued to be a showcase for the sport's most electrifying athletes, with memorable performances by Dwight Howard, Nate Robinson, and Aaron Gordon, among others.

While the high-flying dunkers of basketball may not always be the most well-rounded players, their aerial exploits have left an indelible mark on the sport. These athletes have pushed the boundaries of what is possible on the court, inspiring awe and admiration in fans and fellow players alike. Their gravity-defying feats testify to the power of human potential, and their legacy will continue to inspire future generations of basketball players to reach for the sky.

The Playmakers: Point Guards Who Defined the Game

In basketball's fast-paced, high-scoring world, the point guard position is often considered the court's most crucial and demanding role. As the primary ball handlers and decision-makers, point guards orchestrate the offense, set up plays, and create scoring opportunities for their teammates. This section will delve into the careers and contributions of some of the most iconic playmakers in basketball history, whose exceptional skills, vision, and leadership have left an indelible mark on the sport.

The story of basketball's greatest playmakers begins with Bob Cousy, the original "Houdini of the Hardwood." Cousy's dazzling ball-handling skills and innovative passing techniques revolutionized the point guard position in the 1950s, paving the way for future generations of floor generals. As a six-time NBA champion and 13-time All-Star, Cousy's impact on the game is undeniable, and his name remains synonymous with the art of playmaking.

Another legendary point guard who redefined the position is Earvin "Magic" Johnson. Standing at 6'9", Magic's unique size, speed, and court vision allowed him to dominate the game in ways never seen before. His fierce rivalry with Larry Bird and the Boston Celtics throughout the 1980s captivated fans and elevated the NBA to new heights. Magic's five championships, three MVP awards, and 12 All-Star appearances testify to his greatness and influence on the game.

In the 1990s, John Stockton emerged as one of the most prolific playmakers in NBA history. Known for his precision passing and uncanny ability to read the defense, Stockton became the all-time leader in assists and steals. In addition, his partnership with power forward Karl Malone, known as the "Stockton-to-Malone" connection, remains one of the most iconic duos in basketball history.

The modern era of basketball has also seen its fair share of exceptional point guards. Steve Nash, a two-time MVP, dazzled fans with his creativity and pinpoint accuracy, while Jason Kidd's all-around skills and basketball IQ earned him a spot among the all-time greats. More recently, players like Chris Paul, Stephen Curry, and Russell Westbrook have continued to push the boundaries of the point guard position, showcasing an array of scoring, passing, and defensive talents that have captivated fans and inspired the next generation of playmakers.

While each of these legendary point guards brought their unique style and skillset to the game, they all shared a common trait: an unwavering commitment to making their teammates better. Through their exceptional vision, unselfish play, and ability to control the game's tempo, these playmakers have left an indelible mark on basketball and set the standard for what it means to be a true floor general.

As we continue to celebrate the achievements and contributions of basketball's greatest legends, let us not forget the importance of the playmakers – the court kings who have defined the game through their leadership, creativity, and relentless pursuit of excellence.

Sharpshooters: The Greatest Shooters in Basketball History

In the fast-paced, high-scoring world of basketball, the ability to consistently make shots from beyond the arc or sink a mid-range jumper is a skill that can elevate a player to legendary status. These sharpshooters have left an indelible mark on the sport with their unwavering focus and impeccable shooting form. In this section, we will delve into the careers and accomplishments of the greatest shooters in basketball history, whose prowess on the court has earned them a place among the Court Kings.

The art of shooting a basketball is a delicate balance of power, precision, and timing. It requires countless hours of practice, an innate understanding of the game, and unshakable confidence in one's abilities. The players we will discuss in this section have mastered and redefined this art, setting new standards for what it means to be a sharpshooter in basketball.

One must mention the legendary Larry Bird in basketball history to discuss the greatest shooters. Known for his incredible shooting range and clutch performances, Bird was a three-time NBA champion, three-time MVP, and a 12-time All-Star during his illustrious career with the Boston Celtics. His ability to make seemingly impossible shots under pressure earned him the nickname "Larry Legend," His shooting prowess continues to inspire players today.

Another iconic sharpshooter is Reggie Miller, who spent his 18-year career with the Indiana Pacers. Miller was known for his quick release and deadly accuracy from beyond the arc, making him one of the most feared shooters in NBA history. He was a five-time All-Star and is currently ranked second in all-time three-pointers made, a testament to his incredible skill and longevity in the league.

In recent years, basketball has witnessed the rise of Stephen Curry, a player who has revolutionized the sport with his unprecedented shooting abilities. Curry, a two-time MVP and three-time NBA champion with the Golden State Warriors has shattered numerous shooting records, including the most three-pointers made in a single season. In addition, his unique combination of ball-handling skills, court vision, and shooting range has earned him the title of the greatest shooter in basketball history by many experts and fans.

Other notable sharpshooters in basketball history include Ray Allen, the all-time leader in three-pointers made, and the versatile Dirk Nowitzki, who revolutionized the power forward position with his exceptional shooting skills. These players and countless others have left an indelible mark on the sport, showcasing the importance of shooting prowess in basketball.

In conclusion, the greatest shooters in basketball history have dazzled fans with their incredible skills and played a pivotal role in shaping the sport as we know it today. Their unwavering dedication to perfecting their craft, innate talent, and passion for the game has earned them a place among the Court Kings. As the sport continues to evolve, the legacy of these sharpshooters will undoubtedly inspire future generations of basketball players to reach for greatness on the court.

The Big Men: Dominant Centers and Power Forwards

In basketball, the big men have always held a special place. With their imposing physical presence and unmatched skills, these towering giants have dominated the paint and left an indelible mark on the sport. This section will delve into the careers and contributions of some of basketball history's most dominant centers and power forwards.

The big men have always been the backbone of any successful basketball team. They are the ones who control the paint, grab rebounds, block shots, and score points in the post. Their sheer size and strength make them a force to be reckoned with, and their impact on the game is undeniable.

One of the first dominant big men in basketball history was George Mikan, who played for the Minneapolis Lakers in the 1940s and 1950s. Standing 6'10", Mikan pioneered the sport, using his height and skill to dominate the competition. He was a five-time NBA champion and four-time All-Star, and his influence on the game can still be felt today.

Another legendary big man was Wilt Chamberlain, who played in the NBA from 1959 to 1973. Chamberlain was a true physical specimen, standing at 7'1" and possessing incredible athleticism. He is best known for his record-setting 100-point game in 1962, a feat that has never been matched. Chamberlain was a two-time NBA champion, four-time MVP, and 13-time All-Star.

Bill Russell played for the Boston Celtics from 1956 to 1969 and was another dominant center. Russell was known for his incredible defensive prowess, leading the league in multiple rebounds and blocked shots. He was a key component of the Celtics' dynasty, winning an astounding 11 NBA championships in his 13-year career. Russell was a five-time MVP and 12-time All-Star.

Recently, Shaquille O'Neal, Tim Duncan, and Hakeem Olajuwon have carried on the tradition of dominant big men. O'Neal, a 7'1" center, was a force of nature in the paint, using his size and strength to overpower opponents. He was a four-time NBA champion, three-time Finals MVP, and 15-time All-Star.

Tim Duncan, known as "The Big Fundamental," was a power

forward who played for the San Antonio Spurs from 1997 to 2016. Duncan was known for his quiet demeanor and fundamentally sound game, which led to five NBA championships, two MVP awards, and 15 All-Star appearances.

Hakeem Olajuwon, a Nigerian-American center, played for the Houston Rockets from 1984 to 2001. Olajuwon was known for his incredible footwork and agility, which earned him the nickname "The Dream." He was a two-time NBA champion, one-time MVP, and 12-time All-Star.

These dominant centers and power forwards have left an indelible mark on basketball. Their size, skill, and athleticism have allowed them to control the paint and lead their teams to victory. As the game continues to evolve, the legacy of these big men will undoubtedly inspire future generations of basketball players to reach for greatness.

The Two-Way Stars: Legends Known for Their Offensive and Defensive Prowess

In basketball, some players excel on the offensive end, and some dominate on the court's defensive side. However, a rare breed of legends has emerged over the years who have managed to master both aspects of the game. These two-way stars have left an indelible mark on the sport, showcasing their ability to score points, create plays, and shut down their opponents with equal finesse. This section will delve into the careers of some of the most exceptional two-way stars in basketball history.

One must mention the legendary Michael Jordan to discuss two-way stars. Widely regarded as the greatest basketball player of all time, Jordan's offensive prowess is well-documented, with ten scoring titles and a career average of 30.1 points per game. However, his defensive skills were equally impressive, as he was a nine-time NBA All-Defensive First Team selection and the 1988 NBA Defensive Player of the Year. Jordan's ability to excel on both ends of the court made him a nightmare for opposing teams and set the standard for future two-way stars.

Another iconic two-way player is the "Big Fundamental," Tim

Duncan. The San Antonio Spurs legend was known for his quiet demeanor and fundamentally sound game, allowing him to dominate offensively and defensively. Duncan was a 15-time All-NBA selection and a 15-time NBA All-Defensive Team selection, showcasing his consistency and excellence in both aspects of the game. His ability to score, rebound, and defend made him one of the most complete players in NBA history.

In more recent times, the NBA has seen the rise of two-way stars like Kawhi Leonard and LeBron James. Leonard, known for his stoic demeanor and massive hands, has become one of the premier defenders in the league, winning two NBA Defensive Player of the Year awards. His offensive game has also blossomed, as he has developed into a reliable scorer and clutch performer, leading the Toronto Raptors to their first NBA championship in 2019. LeBron James, on the other hand, has been a dominant force in the league for nearly two decades. His incredible athleticism, court vision, and scoring ability have made him one of the most potent offensive weapons in NBA history. However, his defensive skills, including chase-down blocks and timely steals, have also been crucial in his teams' successes, making him a true two-way star.

These two-way legends have excelled individually and led their teams to championships, proving that a balanced game is essential for success in basketball. Their ability to impact the game on both ends of the court has set them apart from their peers and solidified their status as some of the greatest players ever to grace the hardwood.

As we continue to witness the evolution of basketball, it is clear that the importance of two-way stars will only grow. Contributing offensively and defensively is invaluable in today's fast-paced, high-scoring game. The legends mentioned in this section have paved the way for future generations, inspiring young players to develop a well-rounded game and strive for greatness on both ends of the court.

International Icons: The Global Impact of Basketball Legends

Basketball has transcended borders and becomes a global phenomenon, largely thanks to its international icons' incredible talent and charisma. These players have significantly impacted the NBA and the sport itself and have inspired millions of fans and aspiring athletes worldwide. This section will explore the stories and contributions of some of the most influential international basketball legends.

One of the first international players to make a splash in the NBA was Hakeem Olajuwon, a Nigerian-American center who played for the Houston Rockets. Known as "The Dream," Olajuwon's exceptional footwork, shot-blocking ability, and scoring prowess made him one of the most dominant big men in the league. His success in the NBA paved the way for other African players, such as Dikembe Mutombo and Manute Bol, to showcase their talents on the world stage.

Another international icon who revolutionized the game is Lithuanian center Arvydas Sabonis. Despite joining the NBA later in his career, Sabonis's incredible passing skills, basketball IQ, and shooting ability made him a force to be reckoned with. His success in the league helped popularize the concept of the "stretch big," a center or power forward who can shoot from beyond the arc, which has become a crucial aspect of modern basketball.

Arguably the most famous international basketball player of all time is Dirk Nowitzki, a German power forward who spent his entire 21-year career with the Dallas Mavericks. Nowitzki's unique combination of size, shooting touch, and footwork made him one of the most challenging players to defend. His signature one-legged fadeaway jump shot became a staple of his game and is now emulated by players worldwide. Nowitzki's impact on the sport extends beyond his on-court accomplishments. He has inspired a new generation of European players, such as Kristaps Porzingis and Luka Dončić, to pursue their NBA dreams.

China's Yao Ming is another international legend who left an indelible mark on the sport. Standing at 7'6", Yao was imposing on the court, but his soft touch, shooting range, and passing ability truly set him apart. Yao's success in the NBA helped popularize basketball in China, leading to a surge in the sport's popularity and the development of future Chinese stars like Yi Jianlian and Zhou Qi.

The global impact of basketball legends is not limited to players alone. Coaches like Serbia's Željko Obradović and Lithuania's Jonas Kazlauskas have made significant contributions to the sport by leading their national teams to numerous international titles and sharing their basketball knowledge with players and coaches worldwide.

In conclusion, the international icons of basketball have played a crucial role in shaping the sport's global landscape. Their unique talents, charisma, and dedication to the game have inspired countless fans and aspiring athletes worldwide. As basketball grows in popularity, we can expect to see even more international legends emerge, further solidifying the sport's status as a truly global phenomenon.

The Coaches: Masterminds Behind the Success of Basketball Greats

Behind every great basketball player, there is often an equally great coach who has helped shape and guide their career. These game masterminds have honed their players' skills and developed innovative strategies and tactics that have left an indelible mark on the sport. In this section, we will delve into the lives and careers of some of the most influential and successful coaches in basketball history, who have played a pivotal role in the success of their teams and the legends they have mentored.

One cannot discuss basketball coaching legends without mentioning Phil Jackson, the "Zen Master." With an astounding 11 NBA championships, Jackson is regarded as one of the greatest coaches ever. His unique approach to coaching, which incorporated elements of Zen Buddhism and Native American spirituality, helped him connect with his players on a deeper level. This, in turn, allowed him to get the best out of superstars like Michael Jordan, Scottie Pippen, Kobe Bryant, and Shaquille O'Neal. Jackson's triangle offense, which emphasized ball movement and teamwork, revolutionized the game and contributed to the success of the Chicago Bulls and the Los Angeles Lakers.

Another coaching icon is the late Red Auerbach, who led the Boston Celtics to an incredible nine NBA championships during his tenure. Auerbach was known for his shrewd personnel decisions and ability to motivate and inspire his players. He was a master at exploiting his roster's strengths, which included legends like Bill Russell, Bob Cousy, and John Havlicek. Auerbach's emphasis on teamwork and selflessness laid the foundation for the Celtics' enduring success and established the franchise as one of the most storied in the history of the NBA.

Pat Riley, the slicked-back, Armani suit-wearing coach, is another name that stands out in the annals of basketball coaching history. With five NBA championships to his name, Riley's coaching career spanned three decades and saw him lead the "Showtime" Los Angeles Lakers, the gritty New York Knicks, and the star-studded Miami Heat. Riley's coaching philosophy centered around hard work, discipline, and a relentless pursuit of excellence. His ability to adapt to different teams and eras of the game is a testament to his basketball acumen and versatility as a coach.

Gregg Popovich, the no-nonsense coach of the San Antonio Spurs, has also left an indelible mark on the sport. With five NBA championships and a reputation for developing unheralded players into stars, Popovich's coaching style is characterized by his emphasis on fundamentals, selflessness, and strong team culture. In addition, his ability to adapt to the changing landscape of the NBA and his knack for identifying and nurturing international talent has made him one of the most respected figures in the basketball world.

These coaching legends and many others have played a crucial role in shaping the careers of the basketball greats we admire today. Their innovative strategies, motivational techniques, and unwavering commitment to excellence have led their teams to victory and impacted basketball. So, as we celebrate the Court Kings who have dazzled us with their skills and achievements, let us also pay tribute to the masterminds who have guided them to greatness.

Record Breakers: Unforgettable Achievements and Milestones

In the world of basketball, records are meant to be broken. However, some achievements and milestones stand the test of time, leaving an indelible mark on the sport's history. These record-breakers have pushed the boundaries of what was once possible, inspiring awe and admiration from fans and fellow players alike. In this section, we will delve into the impressive accomplishments of the Court Kings, whose extraordinary feats have etched their names in the annals of basketball legend.

One must mention the name Wilt Chamberlain before discussing basketball records. The towering center, known as "The Big Dipper," set numerous records during his illustrious career, many of which still stand today. His most famous achievement came on March 2, 1962, when he scored an astounding 100 points in a single game, a feat that has never been replicated. Chamberlain also holds the record for the most rebounds in a game, with 55, and the highest career scoring average, at 30.1 points per game.

Another legendary figure who shattered records is Michael Jordan, widely regarded as the greatest basketball player of all time. Jordan's scoring prowess is well-documented, as he holds the record for the most points scored in a single playoff game, with 63, and the highest career playoff scoring average, at 33.4 points per game. Jordan's ten scoring titles and five MVP awards underscore his dominance in the NBA.

In recent years, new stars have emerged to challenge the records set by their predecessors. LeBron James has steadily climbed the ranks of the all-time scoring list, currently sitting in third place and poised to surpass Kareem Abdul-Jabbar's record of 38,387 points potentially. James also holds the record for the most consecutive playoff appearances with 14, showcasing his remarkable consistency and longevity in the league.

Sharpshooters have also left their mark on the record books, with players like Ray Allen and Reggie Miller setting the standard for three-point shooting. Allen currently holds the record for the most career three-pointers made, with 2,973. Miller's clutch shooting in the playoffs earned him the nickname "Knick Killer." In recent years, Stephen Curry has emerged as a threat to these records, as his incredible shooting range and accuracy have redefined how the game is played.

Lastly, we must acknowledge the defensive stalwarts who have made their presence felt on the court. Bill Russell, the centerpiece of the Boston Celtics dynasty in the 1960s, holds the record for the most championships won by a player, with 11 titles in 13 seasons. Russell's shot-blocking and rebounding prowess set the standard for future defensive greats like Hakeem Olajuwon, who holds the record for the most career blocked shots with 3,830.

These record-breakers have etched their names in basketball history and raised the bar for future generations of players. Their exceptional achievements and milestones testify to their talent, hard work, and dedication to the sport. As the game continues to evolve, we can only imagine what new records will be set and which future legends will emerge to challenge the feats of the Court Kings.

The Legacy: How Basketball Legends Inspire Future Generations

The impact of basketball legends extends far beyond the court, as their legacies inspire and motivate future generations of players and fans alike. These Court Kings have not only left an indelible mark on the sport but have also played a significant role in shaping the lives of countless individuals who look up to them as role models and icons.

One of the most profound ways basketball legends inspire future generations is through their relentless work ethic and dedication to the sport. The stories of these players spending countless hours in the gym, perfecting their craft, and pushing their bodies to the limit serve as a testament to the power of hard work and perseverance. Young players who aspire to reach the same heights as their heroes are motivated to emulate their commitment and discipline, understanding that success in basketball, as in life, is earned and not given.

Another aspect of the legacy left by basketball legends is the way they have broken barriers and transcended the sport. Players like Bill

Russell, who fought against racial discrimination and became the first African American coach in the NBA, or Yao Ming, who brought the game to new heights in China, have paved the way for future generations of diverse players to pursue their dreams in the sport. In addition, these trailblazers have shown that basketball is a global game, capable of uniting people from all walks of life and providing opportunities for growth and success.

The on-court achievements of basketball legends also serve as a source of inspiration for future generations. Records set and milestones reached by these players provide tangible goals for young athletes to strive for, pushing them to reach their full potential. Moreover, the unforgettable moments created by these legends – from game-winning shots to gravity-defying dunks – have become etched in the collective memory of basketball fans, fueling the dreams and aspirations of those who hope to create their own memorable moments on the court.

Basketball legends have also used their platforms to give back to their communities and make a positive impact off the court. Through charitable endeavors, mentorship programs, and youth basketball camps, these players have demonstrated the importance of using one's success and influence to uplift others. This aspect of their legacy teaches future generations the value of compassion, empathy, and social responsibility, qualities essential for success in basketball and life.

In conclusion, the legacy of basketball legends goes far beyond their on-court accomplishments. These Court Kings have inspired future generations through their work ethic, barrier-breaking achievements, unforgettable moments, and commitment to giving back. As young players and fans look up to these icons, they are reminded of the power of hard work, perseverance, and the importance of using one's success to impact the world positively. The enduring influence of these legends ensures that the spirit of the game will continue to thrive and evolve as new generations of players strive to leave their mark on the sport.

The Enduring Impact of the Court Kings

As we reach the end of our journey through the world of basketball legends, it is essential to reflect on the enduring impact these Court Kings have had on the sport and the world at large. These exceptional athletes have left their mark on the basketball court and transcended the game, inspiring generations of fans and players alike.

The Court Kings have shown us that basketball is more than just a game; it is a platform for self-expression, creativity, and unity. These legends have pushed the boundaries of what is possible on the court through their incredible skills, relentless work ethic, and unwavering passion for the sport. They have redefined the game, setting new standards for excellence and leaving a lasting legacy that continues to shape the future of basketball.

Their impact goes beyond sports; they have used their fame and influence to make a difference in the world. Many of these legends have become philanthropists, activists, and role models, using their success to give back to their communities and support important causes. They have shown us that greatness is not only measured by the number of points scored or championships won but also by the positive impact one can have on the lives of others.

The stories of these Court Kings serve as a testament to the power of perseverance, determination, and resilience. They have faced adversity, overcome obstacles, and defied the odds to achieve greatness. Their journeys remind us that success is not handed to us; it is earned through hard work, dedication, and an unwavering belief in oneself.

As we celebrate the achievements of these basketball legends, we must also recognize the sport's role in shaping their lives and the lives of countless others. Basketball can bring people together, transcending borders, languages, and cultures. It is a universal language that unites us all, fostering a sense of camaraderie and belonging that is truly unique.

In conclusion, the enduring impact of the Court Kings cannot be overstated. They have forever changed the landscape of basketball, leaving an indelible mark on the sport and the world. Their stories of triumph, perseverance, and passion will continue to inspire future generations of athletes and fans as a reminder of the incredible potential within each of us.

As we look to the future, we can only imagine the new legends that will emerge, the records that will be shattered, and the boundaries that will be pushed. But one thing is sure: the legacy of the Court Kings will live on as their spirit and passion for the game continue to shape the future of basketball and inspire us all to strive for greatness.

5
THE GRIDIRON GREATS: FOOTBALL LEGENDS

Gridiron Football Clash

The roar of the crowd, the clash of helmets, and the thrill of victory define the world of football. A game that has captured the hearts and minds of millions, football has given rise to some of the most iconic and unforgettable legends in sports history. These titans of the turf have left an indelible mark on the game and have inspired generations of fans and players alike with their incredible feats of athleticism, skill, and determination.

This chapter will delve into the lives and careers of the greatest football legends who have ever graced the gridiron. From the masterminds who orchestrated the most awe-inspiring plays to the fearless warriors who battled in the trenches, these heroes have shaped the game as we know it today. Their stories are a testament to the power of perseverance, the importance of teamwork, and the sheer love of the game.

As we journey through the annals of football history, we will explore the various positions and roles that have contributed to making these legends. From the quarterback kings who have commanded their teams with precision and poise to the running backs who have defied the odds with their speed and power, each position has unique challenges and triumphs. We will also pay homage to the unsung heroes of the game – the offensive and defensive linemen who have fought tooth and nail in the trenches, the linebackers who have served as the heart and soul of the defense, and the secondary who have stood as the last line of defense against the opposition.

In addition, we will examine the impact of the coaches who have guided these legends to greatness and the most memorable moments that have defined the game of football. From the iconic plays that have left fans breathless to the nail-biting finishes that have gone down in history, these moments serve as a reminder of the sheer excitement and unpredictability of the game.

As we celebrate the enduring legacy of these football legends, we invite you to join us in reliving their greatest triumphs and honoring their contributions to the sport we all love. So, strap on your helmet, lace up your cleats, and prepare to be inspired by the titans of the turf – the gridiron greats who have forever changed the game of football.

The Quarterback Kings: Masterminds of the Game

In the high-stakes world of professional football, the quarterback is the undisputed leader and mastermind of the game. These kings of the gridiron possess an unparalleled combination of intelligence, athleticism, and poise, orchestrating their team's offensive strategy with the precision of a maestro. In this section, we will delve into the lives and careers of some of the most legendary quarterbacks to ever grace the field, exploring their unique talents and their indelible impact on the sport.

The pantheon of quarterback greats is headlined by names such as Joe Montana, Johnny Unitas, Tom Brady, and Peyton Manning. These iconic figures have not only shattered records and redefined the position but have also inspired generations of fans and players alike with their unwavering commitment to excellence.

Joe Montana, known as "Joe Cool" for his calm demeanor under pressure, led the San Francisco 49ers to four Super Bowl victories and was named Super Bowl MVP three times. His uncanny ability to read defenses and make split-second decisions earned him a reputation as one of the most clutch performers in NFL history.

Johnny Unitas, often called "The Golden Arm," was a trailblazer for the modern quarterback. With his pinpoint accuracy and innovative play-calling, Unitas revolutionized the passing game and set numerous records during his illustrious career with the Baltimore Colts.

In the contemporary era, Tom Brady and Peyton Manning have carried the torch as the preeminent quarterbacks of their generation. Brady, a six-time Super Bowl champion and three-time league MVP, has become synonymous with winning. At the same time, Manning's cerebral approach to the game and mastery of the no-huddle offense earned him five MVP awards and two Super Bowl titles.

Beyond their impressive statistics and accolades, these quarterback kings have left an indelible mark on the game through their leadership and ability to elevate the play of their teammates. In addition, they have repeatedly demonstrated that the quarterback position is about more than just throwing touchdowns; it's about having the mental fortitude to command a huddle, the vision to dissect a defense, and the resilience to bounce back from adversity.

As we continue to marvel at the exploits of these gridiron greats, it is important to remember that their success was not achieved in isolation. Behind every legendary quarterback is a supporting cast of talented teammates, dedicated coaches, and innovative offensive schemes that have allowed them to flourish. In the following sections, we will explore the contributions of these unsung heroes and examine the various components that have shaped the careers of our quarterback kings.

In conclusion, the quarterback position embodies the strategic and competitive spirit that defines the sport of football. The legends we have discussed in this section have excelled at their craft and left an indelible mark on the game's history. Their stories of triumph and perseverance testify to the power of hard work, dedication, and an unwavering belief in one's abilities. As we celebrate the achievements of these gridiron greats, we are reminded of the enduring appeal of football and the timeless allure of the quarterback kings who have ruled the sport.

The Running Back Revolution: Speed and Power Unleashed

The game of football has evolved tremendously over the years, and one position that has seen a significant transformation is the running back. The running back revolution has been characterized by a combination of speed, power, and agility, leaving fans in awe and opponents grasping at air. In this section, we will delve into the world of these gridiron gladiators, exploring their unique skill sets and their impact on the sport.

The early days of football saw running backs primarily used as battering rams, with their main objective being to pound the ball through the defensive line. However, as the game evolved, so did the role of the running back. The revolution began with the emergence of players like Jim Brown, who combined brute strength with breakaway speed, setting the stage for future generations of versatile running backs.

The 1970s and 1980s saw the rise of running backs who were powerful and possessed the agility and finesse to elude defenders. Players like Walter Payton, Earl Campbell, and Eric Dickerson redefined the position, showcasing their ability to change direction on a dime and leave defenders in their wake. These gridiron greats demonstrated that running backs could be more than just powerhouses; they could be game-changers with speed and elusiveness.

As the game continued to evolve, so did the running back position. The 1990s and 2000s saw the emergence of dual-threat running backs who were equally adept at running the ball and catching passes out of the backfield. Players like Marshall Faulk, LaDainian Tomlinson, and Brian Westbrook epitomized this new breed of running back, forcing defenses to account for their versatility and creating mismatches all over the field.

The current generation of running backs has taken the position to new heights, with players like Adrian Peterson, Le'Veon Bell, and Saquon Barkley showcasing a blend of power, speed, and agility that is nothing short of awe-inspiring. These athletes can break tackles, outrun defenders, and leap over would-be tacklers, making them a nightmare for opposing defenses.

The running back revolution has not only changed how the position is played but has also had a profound impact on the game of football. The versatility and athleticism of modern running backs have forced defenses to adapt, creating new defensive schemes and strategies to counter these dynamic playmakers. Additionally, the rise of dual-threat running backs has increased emphasis on pass-catching skills for the position, further expanding the role of running backs in the modern game.

In conclusion, the running back revolution has been a thrilling and transformative journey, marked by the emergence of some of the most talented and exciting athletes the sport has ever seen. These gridiron greats have redefined the position, unleashing a potent combination of speed and power that has forever changed the football landscape. As we continue to marvel at the exploits of today's running backs, we can only imagine what the future holds for this ever-evolving position.

Wide Receivers: The Art of the Impossible Catch

In the high-stakes world of professional football, wide receivers are the artists who paint the field with breathtaking athleticism and skill displays. These gridiron greats have an uncanny ability to make the impossible catch, turning the tide of a game instantly and leaving fans in awe. In this section, we will delve into the world of wide receivers, exploring the qualities that set them apart and celebrating the legends who have left an indelible mark on the sport.

Wide receivers are the epitome of grace under pressure. They must possess lightning-fast speed, razor-sharp reflexes, and an unwavering focus to excel in their position. As they sprint down the field, they must keep their eyes on the ball, anticipate its trajectory, and adjust their route accordingly, all while evading the clutches of the opposing team's defenders. It is a delicate dance that requires a unique blend of physical prowess and mental fortitude.

The legends of the wide receiver position are those who have mastered this art form, making catches that defy logic and inspire generations of fans. One such legend is Jerry Rice, widely regarded as the greatest wide receiver of all time. Over his illustrious 20-year career, Rice set numerous records, including most career receptions, receiving yards, and receiving touchdowns. His ability to make seemingly impossible catches, often in the most crucial moments of a game, earned him the nickname "World," as in, "he could catch anything in the world."

Another iconic wide receiver is Randy Moss, whose combination of size, speed, and leaping ability made him a nightmare for opposing defenses. Moss's penchant for making acrobatic, one-handed catches earned him the moniker "The Freak," His highlight reel is filled with jaw-dropping plays showcasing his extraordinary talent.

The art of the impossible catch is not limited to the past, as current wide receivers continue to push the boundaries of what is possible on the gridiron. DeAndre Hopkins, Julio Jones, and Odell Beckham Jr. are just a few of the modern-day maestros who have made their mark with gravity-defying catches that leave fans and opponents shaking their heads in disbelief.

While the wide receiver position is often associated with flashy plays and attention-grabbing antics, the true essence of the role lies in the ability to make the impossible catch. This skill separates the good from the great and cements the legacy of the legends who have graced the gridiron. As we continue to marvel at the feats of these extraordinary athletes, we are reminded of the beauty and artistry that lies at the heart of the sport of football.

The Offensive Line: Unsung Heroes of the Gridiron

In the high-octane world of football, where speed, agility, and power often take center stage, it is easy to overlook the importance of the offensive line. These unsung gridiron heroes may not always make the highlight reels or grace the covers of sports magazines, but their contributions to the game are invaluable. The offensive line is the backbone of any successful football team, providing the foundation for the offense. In this section, we will delve into the world of the offensive line, exploring the roles, responsibilities, and skills that make these players the true titans of the turf.

The offensive line comprises five players: the center, two guards, and two tackles. Each position has unique responsibilities, but their collective goal is to protect the quarterback and create running lanes for the running backs. The center is the anchor of the line, responsible for snapping the ball to the quarterback and making crucial line calls to ensure proper blocking assignments. Guards, positioned on either side of the center, are tasked with blocking defensive linemen and linebackers, while tackles, the outermost players on the line, protect the quarterback's blindside and open up running lanes on the edge.

The offensive line's success hinges on a combination of physical prowess, mental acuity, and seamless communication. These players must possess the strength to overpower their opponents, the agility to adjust to the ever-changing landscape of the line of scrimmage, and the intelligence to recognize and react to defensive schemes. In addition, communication is paramount, as a single missed assignment can result in a devastating sack or a stuffed running play.

While the offensive line may not garner the same level of attention as their skill position counterparts, their impact on the game is undeniable. A dominant offensive line can control the game's tempo, wearing down the opposing defense and allowing the offense to dictate the flow of play. Conversely, a porous offensive line can cripple an offense, leaving the quarterback vulnerable to constant pressure and stifling the running game.

Throughout the history of football, there have been numerous offensive linemen who have left an indelible mark on the game. Players like Anthony Munoz, John Hannah, and Bruce Matthews exemplify the perfect blend of power, agility, and intelligence that defines the offensive line. These legends paved the way for the modern generation of linemen, who continue to push the boundaries of what is possible on the gridiron.

In conclusion, the offensive line is the unsung hero of the football world. These players may only sometimes receive the accolades and recognition they deserve, but their contributions to the game are invaluable. So the next time you watch a football game, take a moment to appreciate the skill and dedication of the offensive line, the true titans of the turf.

The Defensive Line: The Wall of Intimidation

In the high-stakes football game, the defensive line stands as a formidable force, a wall of intimidation that strikes fear into the hearts of their opponents. These gridiron gladiators are the first line of defense, stopping the opposing team's offensive advances. With a combination of brute strength, agility, and strategic thinking, the defensive line has produced some of the most legendary players in history.

The defensive line comprises defensive tackles and defensive ends, each with unique roles and responsibilities. Defensive tackles, often the largest and strongest players on the field, are responsible for clogging up the middle of the line, preventing running backs from breaking through and disrupting the quarterback's plans. Their sheer size and power make them a force to be reckoned with as they push through the offensive line to wreak havoc in the backfield.

Defensive ends, on the other hand, are typically leaner and faster than their tackle counterparts. Their primary objective is to rush the quarterback, using their speed and agility to evade blockers and bring down the opposing team's signal-caller. In addition, they must also contain the outside running game, forcing the ball carrier back toward the center of the field, where their teammates can swarm in for the tackle.

Throughout the history of football, the defensive line has been home to some of the most iconic and intimidating players the sport has ever seen. Legends like Reggie White, Deacon Jones, and Bruce Smith terrorized quarterbacks with their relentless pursuit and bone-crushing sacks. Meanwhile, defensive tackles like "Mean" Joe Greene, Warren Sapp, and Vince Wilfork anchored their teams' defenses, clogging up running lanes and making life miserable for opposing offenses.

The success of a defensive line is not solely measured in sacks and tackles for loss but also in the intangible impact they have on the game. A dominant defensive line can dictate the tempo of a match, forcing the opposing offense to alter their game plan and make costly mistakes. The psychological warfare waged by these gridiron warriors can be just as important as their physical prowess, as they seek to instill fear and doubt in the minds of their adversaries.

In conclusion, the defensive line is essential to any successful football team. These gridiron greats, the wall of intimidation, have left an indelible mark on the sport, creating a legacy of dominance and fear that will be remembered for generations. As fans, we can only marvel at their incredible feats of strength, speed, and determination as they continue to shape the game we know and love.

Linebackers: The Heart and Soul of the Defense

In the high-stakes football game, the linebackers are the heart and soul of the defense. These versatile athletes possess a unique combination of size, speed, and intelligence, making them the ultimate defensive weapon. Tasked with stopping the run, pressuring the quarterback, and covering receivers, linebackers are the glue that holds the defense together. In this section, we will explore the qualities that make linebackers so vital to the success of a football team and celebrate some of the greatest ever to play the position.

Linebackers are often called the "quarterbacks of the defense" due to their leadership role on the field. They are responsible for reading the offense, making adjustments, and ensuring that their teammates are in the correct position to make a play. This requires an in-depth understanding of the game and the ability to communicate effectively with their fellow defenders.

One of the most important attributes of a great linebacker is their ability to stop the run. This requires a combination of size, strength, and agility, as they must shed blocks from offensive linemen and bring down powerful running backs. Legendary linebackers like Dick Butkus, Ray Lewis, and Mike Singletary were all known for their ferocious tackling and ability to shut down the run game.

In addition to stopping the run, linebackers must be adept at pressuring the quarterback. Blitzing can achieve this, where the linebacker rushes the quarterback to force a hurried throw or sack. Some of history's most feared pass-rushing linebackers include Lawrence Taylor, Derrick Thomas, and Von Miller, who have all left their mark on the game with their relentless pursuit of the quarterback.

Linebackers must also possess the ability to cover receivers in the passing game. This requires a unique blend of speed, agility, and awareness, as they must keep up with fast and elusive pass-catchers. Players like Brian Urlacher, Luke Kuechly, and Bobby Wagner have excelled in this aspect of the game, showcasing their ability to cover large areas of the field and make game-changing interceptions.

Throughout the history of football, there have been many iconic linebackers who have left an indelible mark on the game. Players like Jack Lambert, Ray Nitschke, and Junior Seau embodied the toughness, intensity, and passion that define the position. These gridiron greats made countless game-changing plays and inspired their teammates and fans with their unwavering commitment to the sport.

In conclusion, linebackers are the heart and soul of the defense, providing leadership, versatility, and a relentless drive to succeed. Their unique size, speed, and intelligence make them an invaluable asset to any football team. As we celebrate the gridiron legends, let us not forget the vital role these defensive warriors have played in shaping the game we know and love today.

The Secondary: The Last Line of Defense

In high-stakes football, the secondary is often the last line of defense between the opposing team and the end zone. These skilled athletes are tasked with preventing the opposing team's wide receivers from making game-changing catches and scoring touchdowns. In this section, we will delve into the essential roles played by the secondary, their unique skills, and the legendary players who have left an indelible mark on the game.

The secondary comprises cornerbacks and safeties, each with distinct field responsibilities. Cornerbacks are typically assigned to cover the opposing team's wide receivers, using their speed, agility, and keen instincts to prevent successful pass completions. Safeties, on the other hand, are the last line of defense, providing support to the cornerbacks and linebackers while also keeping an eye on the quarterback's movements. They must possess exceptional awareness and anticipation skills, as they are often responsible for making split-second decisions that can alter the course of the game.

Throughout the history of football, numerous secondary players have etched their names in the annals of gridiron greatness. Deion Sanders, nicknamed "Prime Time" for his penchant for making big plays in crucial moments, is regarded as one of the greatest cornerbacks ever. With his unparalleled speed, agility, and ball-hawking skills,

Sanders was a nightmare for opposing quarterbacks and wide receivers.

Another secondary legend is Ronnie Lott, a hard-hitting safety who struck fear into the hearts of his opponents. Lott's tenacity and ferocious tackling ability made him a force to be reckoned with on the field, and his leadership skills earned him the respect of his teammates and coaches. His impact on the game can still be felt today as aspiring safeties look to emulate his aggressive style of play.

The secondary's importance in the game of football cannot be overstated. As the last line of defense, these athletes must possess a unique combination of physical prowess, mental acuity, and unwavering determination. As a result, they are often the difference-makers in tight games, stepping up to make game-saving interceptions or delivering bone-crushing tackles that swing the momentum in their team's favor.

In conclusion, the secondary is integral to any successful football team. The gridiron legends who have excelled in these positions have left a lasting legacy, inspiring future generations of athletes to push the boundaries of what is possible on the field. As the game continues to evolve, there is no doubt that the secondary will remain a vital component of the sport. The legends who have made their mark in this area will forever be remembered as some of the greatest to grace the gridiron.

Special Teams: The Game Changers

In the high-stakes world of professional football, every play counts, and every yard matters. While the spotlight often shines on the quarterbacks, running backs, and wide receivers, a group of players can make or break a game with a single play: the special teams. These unsung heroes of the gridiron are responsible for some of the most thrilling and game-changing moments in football history. In this section, we will explore the vital role of special teams, the unique skills they bring to the field, and the unforgettable plays that have earned them a place among football's legends.

Special teams comprise diverse players, each with a specific role to play in the game's most critical situations. They include kickers, punters, long snappers, return specialists, and the men who make up the coverage and return units. Together, they are responsible for executing kickoffs, punts, field goals, extra points, and returns – plays that can swing the momentum of a game in an instant.

Kickers and punters may not be the most physically imposing players on the field, but their ability to control field position and put points on the board is invaluable. A clutch field goal or a perfectly placed punt can be the difference between victory and defeat. Legends like Adam Vinatieri, known for his game-winning kicks in the most pressure-packed situations, and Ray Guy, the first punter ever inducted into the Pro Football Hall of Fame, have left an indelible mark on the sport with their skill and poise under pressure.

Return specialists like Devin Hester and Dante Hall possess a unique combination of speed, agility, and vision to navigate through a sea of defenders and find a path to the end zone. Their electrifying returns can ignite a stadium and shift the momentum of a game in a matter of seconds.

The coverage and return units, often composed of players from various positions, are the unsung heroes of special teams. Their relentless pursuit and fearless tackling can prevent big returns, pin opponents deep into their territory, and even create scoring opportunities through blocked kicks or forced fumbles. As a result, players like Steve Tasker, who made a career out of excelling on special teams, have earned their peers and fans' respect and admiration.

Throughout football history, special teams have provided some of the most memorable moments in the sport. From the "Music City Miracle" to the "Immaculate Reception," these game-changing plays have become etched in the annals of gridiron lore. They serve as a reminder that in football, every player, no matter their role, has the potential to make a lasting impact.

In conclusion, the special teams are the game changers of football, often turning the tide of a match with a single play. Their unique skills and unwavering determination make them integral to any successful team. As we celebrate the legends of the gridiron, let us not forget the vital contributions of these unsung heroes, who have left an indelible mark on the sport we love.

The Coaches: Architects of Gridiron Greatness

Behind every great football team lies a mastermind, a strategist who orchestrates the movements and decisions that lead to victory. These architects of gridiron greatness are the coaches, the individuals who mold raw talent into a cohesive unit, instilling discipline, teamwork, and a relentless pursuit of excellence. In this section, we will delve into the lives and careers of some of the most legendary football coaches, exploring their unique approaches to the game and their indelible impact on the sport.

The role of a football coach extends far beyond the sidelines. They are responsible for developing game plans, analyzing opponents, and making crucial in-game adjustments. Their most important task is to inspire and motivate their players, pushing them to reach their full potential. Great coaches possess an uncanny ability to connect with their athletes, fostering a sense of trust and loyalty that translates into on-field success.

One such iconic figure is Vince Lombardi, whose name adorns the trophy awarded to the Super Bowl champion each year. As head coach of the Green Bay Packers in the 1960s, Lombardi led his team to five NFL championships and two Super Bowl victories. His no-nonsense approach and unwavering commitment to excellence set the standard for future coaches. Lombardi's famous quote, "Winning isn't everything. It's the only thing," encapsulates his relentless pursuit of success.

Another coaching legend is Bill Walsh, the innovative mastermind behind the San Francisco 49ers dynasty of the 1980s. Walsh's revolutionary West Coast offense, emphasizing short, precise passing and a solid running game, transformed how football was played. Under his guidance, the 49ers won three Super Bowls and produced some of the most memorable moments in NFL history. Walsh's coaching tree, which includes names like George Seifert, Mike Holmgren, and Andy Reid, is a testament to his lasting influence on the game.

In the modern era, few coaches can rival the success of Bill Belichick, the enigmatic leader of the New England Patriots. With a keen eye for talent and an unmatched ability to adapt his game plan to exploit opponents' weaknesses, Belichick has guided the Patriots to six Super Bowl titles since 2001. His partnership with quarterback Tom Brady, widely regarded as the greatest of all time, has solidified their place in football history.

While these coaches have left an indelible mark on the sport, countless others have contributed to the rich tapestry of football history. From the fiery intensity of Mike Ditka to the calm, cerebral approach of Tony Dungy, each coach brings their unique personality and philosophy to the game. Their passion, dedication, and innovative thinking have shaped the sport we know and love today.

In conclusion, the coaches are the architects of gridiron greatness, the masterminds who transform raw talent into championship-winning teams. Their impact on the sport is immeasurable, as they inspire generations of players and fans with their pursuit of excellence. So, as we celebrate the gridiron legends, let us remember the crucial role these coaches have played in creating the unforgettable moments that define the game of football.

The Most Memorable Moments in Football History

Throughout the storied history of football, countless moments have left fans in awe, inspired generations of players, and etched themselves into the annals of sports legend. These unforgettable moments have transcended the game, becoming part of our cultural fabric and forever shaping how we view the sport. In this section, we will revisit some of the most memorable moments in football history, reliving the excitement, drama, and sheer athletic prowess that has made these instances genuinely iconic.

One such moment is the iconic "Immaculate Reception" during the 1972 AFC Divisional Playoff game between the Pittsburgh Steelers and the Oakland Raiders. With 22 seconds left on the clock and the Steelers trailing 7-6, quarterback Terry Bradshaw launched a desperate pass downfield. The ball ricocheted off a defender and, seemingly out of nowhere, was scooped up by running back Franco Harris, who sprinted into the end zone for a miraculous game-winning touchdown. This improbable play secured the Steelers' victory and marked the beginning of their rise to dominance in the 1970s.

Another unforgettable moment occurred during the 1982 NFC Championship game when San Francisco 49ers quarterback Joe Montana connected with wide receiver Dwight Clark for "The Catch." With less than a minute remaining and the 49ers trailing the Dallas Cowboys 27-21, Montana rolled to his right and lofted a high pass to the back of the end zone. Clark leaped into the air, fingertips outstretched, and miraculously snagged the ball for the game-winning touchdown. This iconic play propelled the 49ers to their first Super Bowl appearance and ignited a dynasty dominating the NFL throughout the 1980s.

No discussion of memorable football moments would be complete without mentioning the "Music City Miracle," which occurred during the 1999 AFC Wild Card game between the Tennessee Titans and the Buffalo Bills. With just 16 seconds remaining and the Titans trailing 16-15, they attempted a seemingly hopeless lateral pass on a kickoff return. In a stunning display of athleticism and improvisation, tight end Frank Wycheck threw a lateral pass across the field to wide receiver Kevin Dyson, who sprinted 75 yards for the game-winning touchdown. This great play sent the Titans to the next round of the playoffs and remained one of the most thrilling moments in NFL history.

Finally, we must acknowledge the legendary "Helmet Catch" from Super Bowl XLII, which pitted the underdog New York Giants against the undefeated New England Patriots. With just over a minute left in the game and the Giants trailing 14-10, quarterback Eli Manning evaded a seemingly sure sack and heaved a desperate pass downfield. Wide receiver David Tyree leaped into the air, trapping the ball against his helmet as he fell to the ground, securing a miraculous catch that kept the Giants' game-winning drive alive. This improbable play set the stage for the Giants' stunning upset victory, derailing the Patriots' bid for a perfect season and cementing its place in football lore.

These moments and countless others have defined the rich history of football and the incredible athletes who have graced the gridiron. They are a testament to the power of determination, skill, and teamwork and will forever be remembered as some of the most memorable moments in football history.

The Enduring Legacy of Football Legends

As we reach the end of our journey through the pantheon of gridiron greats, we must reflect on the enduring legacy these legends have left on football. The game has evolved tremendously from the early days of leather helmets and muddy fields to the modern era of high-tech stadiums and global audiences. Yet, the spirit and passion of these football legends remain a constant, inspiring generation of fans and players alike.

The stories of these football legends are not just about their incredible athletic feats but also about their resilience, determination, and unwavering commitment to the sport. They have faced adversity, overcome obstacles, and defied the odds to etch their names in the annals of football history. Their legacies testify to the power of hard work, dedication, and perseverance.

The impact of these legends extends far beyond the gridiron. They have become role models for countless young athletes, teaching them the importance of sportsmanship, teamwork, and discipline. Through their actions on and off the field, they have demonstrated that the number of touchdowns measures success scored or tackles made and how one conducts oneself in the face of challenges and adversity.

Moreover, the legacy of these football legends has transcended the sport itself, influencing popular culture, fashion, and even language. Phrases like "Hail Mary pass" and "the Immaculate Reception" have become part of our everyday lexicon. At the same time, iconic images of players like Joe Namath and Deion Sanders have graced magazine covers and adorned bedroom walls. The influence of these legends is felt not only in the world of sports but also in the broader cultural landscape.

As we celebrate the achievements of these sports legends, let us also remember the countless others who have contributed to the rich tapestry of football history. From the unsung heroes of the offensive and defensive lines to the trailblazing coaches who have revolutionized the game, each individual has played a crucial role in shaping the sport we know and love today.

In conclusion, the enduring legacy of football legends is a testament to the power of the human spirit and the unyielding pursuit of excellence. As fans, we are privileged to witness the extraordinary feats of these athletes, who have forever changed how we experience and appreciate the game of football. Their stories will continue to inspire and captivate us for generations to come, reminding us that greatness is not only achieved through talent but also through the relentless pursuit of one's dreams.

6

THE ICE WARRIORS: HOCKEY LEGENDS

Ice Hockey Hustle

H ockey, a sport that has captivated the hearts and minds of millions of fans worldwide, has given rise to some of the most legendary athletes in sports history. From its humble beginnings on frozen ponds and makeshift rinks, hockey has evolved into a fast-paced, thrilling game that showcases its players' incredible skill, strength, and determination. The birth of hockey legends can be traced back to the sport's early days when pioneers of the game laid the foundation for the superstars that would follow in their footsteps.

The origins of ice hockey can be traced back to the 19th century when various forms of the game were played in Canada, the United States, and Europe. As the sport gained popularity, it began attracting talented athletes who would become the first hockey legends. These early heroes of the game not only demonstrated exceptional skill on the ice and helped shape the rules and strategies that would define the sport for generations to come.

As hockey continued to grow and evolve, so did the level of competition and the caliber of its players. The introduction of professional leagues, such as the National Hockey League (NHL), provided a platform for the most talented athletes to showcase their abilities and compete against the best. As a result, this era saw the emergence of hockey's most dominant players, who would set records, win championships, and inspire countless fans with their incredible feats on the ice.

Throughout the sport's history, hockey has produced a diverse array of legendary players, each with their unique style and approach to the game. From the lightning-fast reflexes of the goalie greats to the impenetrable defense of the blue-line guardians, these athletes have left an indelible mark on the sport and earned their place in the annals of hockey history. In addition, the playmakers, snipers, enforcers, and captains have all contributed to the game's rich tapestry, demonstrating the many different ways a player can achieve greatness on the ice.

In addition to the individual achievements of these legendary athletes, the sport of hockey has also been shaped by the visionary coaches who have guided their teams to victory. These game masterminds have developed innovative strategies and tactics that have pushed the boundaries of what is possible on the ice, leading their teams to new heights and cementing their place in hockey lore.

The international stage has also played a significant role in the birth of hockey legends, as players worldwide have come together to represent their countries in fierce competition. From the Olympic Games to the World Championships, these global events have showcased the sport's most talented athletes and given rise to some of the most memorable moments in hockey history.

In conclusion, the birth of hockey legends can be traced back to the sport's early days, when pioneers laid the groundwork for the incredible athletes that would follow. Through their skill, determination, and passion for the game, these legendary players have left an enduring legacy that continues to inspire and captivate fans worldwide. As hockey continues to evolve and grow, there is no doubt that new legends will emerge, adding to this beloved game's rich history and tradition.

The Pioneers: Early Hockey Heroes

The history of hockey is filled with legendary players who have left an indelible mark on the sport. Among these greats, the game pioneers stand out as true trailblazers, setting the stage for future hockey heroes. These early hockey icons displayed exceptional skill and talent on the ice and played a crucial role in shaping the game as we know it today. This section will delve into the lives and careers of some of the most influential pioneers in hockey history.

One cannot discuss the early days of hockey without mentioning the legendary Cyclone Taylor. Born in 1884, Frederick Wellington "Cyclone" Taylor was a Canadian professional ice hockey player widely regarded as one of the first true superstars of the sport. With his incredible speed, agility, and scoring prowess, Taylor was a force to be reckoned with on the ice. He played for several teams, including the Ottawa Senators, Vancouver Millionaires, and the Renfrew Creamery Kings. Taylor's impact on the game was immense, and his name remains synonymous with the early days of professional hockey.

Another sports pioneer was the "Flying Frenchman," Newsy Lalonde. Born in 1887, Édouard Cyrille "Newsy" Lalonde was a Canadian professional ice hockey forward who played for the Montreal Canadiens, among other teams. Lalonde was known for his incredible goal-scoring ability, often leading the league in goals during his career. His skill and determination on the ice helped to popularize the sport in Quebec and across Canada, paving the way for future generations of French-Canadian hockey players.

The early days of hockey also saw the rise of the first great goaltender, Georges Vézina. Born in 1887, Vézina was a Canadian professional ice hockey goaltender who played his entire career with the Montreal Canadiens. Nicknamed the "Chicoutimi Cucumber" for his calm demeanor under pressure, Vézina pioneered the goaltending techniques that would become the foundation for future netminders. His exceptional skill and consistency in the crease earned him the honor of having the Vezina Trophy, awarded annually to the NHL's best goaltender, named in his memory.

The contributions of these early hockey heroes extended beyond their on-ice performances. Players like Cyclone Taylor, Newsy Lalonde, and Georges Vézina were instrumental in popularizing the sport, drawing fans to arenas and inspiring countless young players to lace up their skates and hit the ice. Their passion for the game and dedication to their craft laid the groundwork for developing hockey as a major professional sport in North America and worldwide.

In conclusion, hockey pioneers were true trailblazers, setting the stage for the legends that would follow in their footsteps. Their skill, determination, and love for the game helped shape hockey into the thrilling and beloved sport it is today. As we continue to celebrate the achievements of hockey's greatest players, let us not forget the early heroes who paved the way for their success.

The Golden Era: Hockey's Most Dominant Players

The Golden Era of hockey, from the 1950s to the 1980s, was when the sport was graced by some of its most talented and dominant players. These athletes revolutionized the game with their exceptional skills and abilities and left an indelible mark on the hearts of fans and fellow players alike. This section will delve into the lives and careers of some of the most iconic figures from this remarkable period in hockey history.

One must mention the legendary Gordie Howe to discuss the Golden Era. Known as "Mr. Hockey," Howe's career spanned an incredible five decades, and was a force to be reckoned with on the ice. With his unparalleled combination of skill, strength, and longevity, Howe set numerous records, including the most goals, assists, and points in a career, many of which stood for decades. As a result, his name became synonymous with the sport, and his impact on the game is still felt today.

Another titan of the Golden Era was Bobby Orr, a defenseman who revolutionized the position with his offensive prowess. Orr's ability to control the game from the blue line and contribute to his team's attack was extraordinary. He was the first defenseman to lead the league in scoring, accomplishing the feat twice. His iconic "flying goal" in the 1970 Stanley Cup Final remains one of the most memorable moments in hockey history. Orr's career may have been cut short by injuries, but his impact on the game is undeniable.

The Golden Era also saw the rise of the "Broad Street Bullies," the Philadelphia Flyers teams of the 1970s known for their physical and aggressive style of play. Led by captain Bobby Clarke, a tenacious and skilled forward, the Flyers won back-to-back Stanley Cup championships in 1974 and 1975. Clarke's leadership and relentless work ethic, combined with the toughness of players like Dave Schultz and the goaltending of Bernie Parent, made the Flyers a dominant force during this period.

Without mentioning the incomparable Wayne Gretzky, no discussion of the Golden Era would be complete. Known as "The Great One,"

Gretzky's skill, vision, and hockey IQ were unmatched, and he shattered numerous records during his illustrious career. With his incredible playmaking abilities and uncanny knack for scoring, Gretzky led the Edmonton Oilers to four Stanley Cup championships in the 1980s and solidified his status as the greatest player in the sport's history.

Finally, we must acknowledge the contributions of international players during the Golden Era, such as Soviet stars Vladislav Tretiak, Valeri Kharlamov, and Viacheslav Fetisov. These players, along with their teammates on the dominant Soviet national teams of the 1970s and 1980s, showcased a unique and highly skilled hockey brand that captivated fans worldwide. Their performances on the international stage, particularly in the famous 1972 Summit Series and the 1980 "Miracle on Ice," helped to grow the sport globally and inspired a new generation of players.

In conclusion, the Golden Era of hockey was a time of unparalleled talent and unforgettable moments. The legends of this era dominated the game and left a lasting impact on the sport, inspiring countless future players and fans. Their contributions to hockey will forever be remembered and celebrated, as they were the giants upon whose shoulders the sport now stands.

The Goalie Greats: Masters of the Crease

In the fast-paced, high-stakes world of ice hockey, the goaltender is the last line of defense, the net's guardian, and the team's backbone. The pressure on these athletes is immense as they face a barrage of shots, some traveling over 100 miles per hour. The greatest goaltenders in the sport's history have not only withstood this pressure but have thrived under it, earning their place among the pantheon of hockey legends. This section will explore the careers and achievements of some of the most exceptional goalies ever to grace the ice.

Jacques Plante is the first name that comes to mind when discussing the greatest goaltenders of all time. A pioneer in the sport, Plante was the first goalie to regularly wear a mask, revolutionizing the position and paving the way for future generations. His innovative style and exceptional skill led him to win six Stanley Cups with the Montreal Canadiens and seven Vezina Trophies as the league's best goaltender. Plante's impact on the game is still felt today, as his innovations have become standard practice for goaltenders worldwide.

Another legendary figure between the pipes is Terry Sawchuk, whose incredible career spanned over two decades. Sawchuk's remarkable reflexes and ability to read the game made him one of the most dominant goalies of his era. He amassed an astounding 103 shutouts and four Vezina Trophies throughout his career, and his name is etched on the Stanley Cup four times. Unfortunately, Sawchuk's tragic death at 40 only adds to the mystique surrounding his legendary career.

Dominik Hasek, known as "The Dominator," is regarded as one of the most talented and unorthodox goaltenders in the sport's history. Hasek's unique style, which combined incredible flexibility with lightning-fast reflexes, made him nearly impossible to beat. The Czech netminder won six Vezina Trophies and two Hart Trophies as the league's most valuable player, a rare feat for a goaltender. Hasek's international success, including two Olympic gold medals, further cements his status as one of the all-time greats.

Discussion of goaltending legends would only be complete by mentioning Martin Brodeur, the NHL's all-time leader in wins, shutouts, and games played by a goaltender. Brodeur's calm demeanor and exceptional puck-handling skills set him apart from his peers as he redefined the role of the modern goaltender. With three Stanley Cups and four Vezina Trophies, Brodeur's place among the greatest goalies in history is unquestionable.

These are just a few examples of the incredible athletes who have manned the crease throughout the history of ice hockey. Their skill, determination, and ability to perform under pressure have earned them a place among the sport's most revered legends. The legacy of these goaltending greats continues to inspire and influence the next generation of netminders, ensuring that the position remains a vital and celebrated aspect of the game.

The Defensemen: Guardians of the Blue Line

In ice hockey's fast-paced, high-stakes world, defensemen are the unsung heroes who often make the difference between victory and defeat. These skilled athletes protect their team's net and shut down the opposition's offensive threats. As the guardians of the blue line, they must possess a unique combination of physical prowess, tactical acumen, and unyielding determination. This section will pay tribute to the legendary defensemen who have left an indelible mark on the sport with their exceptional performances and unwavering commitment to excellence.

The role of a defenseman in hockey is multifaceted and demanding. They must be adept at blocking shots, delivering bone-crunching body checks, and clearing the puck from their defensive zone. At the same time, they are expected to contribute offensively by making pinpoint passes and launching powerful shots from the blue line. The best defensemen in the sport's history have excelled in all these aspects, showcasing a remarkable blend of skill, strength, and intelligence.

One of the most iconic defensemen of all time is Bobby Orr, who revolutionized the position with his dynamic style of play. Orr's incredible skating ability and offensive instincts allowed him to dominate games like no other defenseman before him. He set numerous records with his trademark end-to-end rushes and unparalleled vision and won two Stanley Cups with the Boston Bruins. Orr's impact on the game is still felt today, as modern defensemen strive to emulate his unique blend of offensive flair and defensive solidity.

Another legendary figure in the pantheon of great defensemen is Doug Harvey, renowned for his exceptional hockey IQ and ability to control the game's pace. Harvey's calm demeanor and precise passing made him a vital cog in the Montreal Canadiens dynasty of the 1950s, during which they won six Stanley Cups. His leadership and poise under pressure earned him the nickname "The General" and cemented his status as one of the all-time greats.

The list of illustrious defensemen would only be complete by mentioning the likes of Ray Bourque, Nicklas Lidstrom, and Scott

Stevens. Bourque's extraordinary consistency and offensive prowess saw him amass an astonishing 1,579 points over his 22-year career, while Lidstrom's impeccable positioning and smooth skating made him a perennial Norris Trophy contender. On the other hand, Stevens was the epitome of a hard-nosed, physical defenseman, striking fear into the hearts of opposing forwards with his thunderous body checks.

In the modern era, defensemen such as Erik Karlsson, Drew Doughty, and Victor Hedman have carried on the legacy of their illustrious predecessors. These players have redefined the position with their exceptional two-way play, combining offensive creativity with defensive responsibility. As the game continues to evolve, there is no doubt that future generations of defensemen will be inspired by the exploits of these ice warriors, who have left an indelible mark on the sport with their unwavering commitment to excellence and their relentless pursuit of victory.

The Playmakers: Architects of the Game

In the fast-paced, high-intensity world of ice hockey, the playmakers are the masterminds who orchestrate the game with precision and finesse. These gifted athletes possess an uncanny ability to read the play, anticipate their opponent's moves, and create scoring opportunities for their teammates. They are the game's architects, crafting intricate plays and setting the stage for unforgettable moments on the ice.

A specific position does not define the role of a playmaker; instead, it is a skill set that transcends traditional boundaries. Playmakers can be found among forwards, defensemen, and even goaltenders. What unites them is their exceptional vision, hockey IQ, and innate understanding of the game's subtleties.

One of the most iconic playmakers in hockey history is Wayne Gretzky, known as "The Great One." Gretzky's extraordinary vision and ability to anticipate plays allowed him to set numerous records, including the most assists in a single season and the most career assists. His innate understanding of the game and his teammates' positioning made him a formidable force on the ice.

Another legendary playmaker is Mario Lemieux, whose size, skill, and finesse earned him the nickname "Le Magnifique." Lemieux's ability to control the puck and create scoring opportunities for his teammates made him one of the most dominant players of his era. Despite facing numerous health challenges throughout his career, Lemieux's impact on the game remains unparalleled.

In recent years, players like Sidney Crosby and Connor McDavid have emerged as the new generation of playmakers. Crosby, known for his incredible hockey sense and vision, has led the Pittsburgh Penguins to multiple Stanley Cup championships. McDavid, often compared to Gretzky for his speed and skill, has quickly established himself as one of the most exciting players in the league.

The playmakers' impact on the game extends beyond their individual achievements. Their ability to elevate the performance of their teammates and create a winning culture is what truly sets them apart. They are the catalysts for their teams' success, inspiring those around them to reach new heights.

As we celebrate the game's architects, it is important to recognize the unique qualities that define a playmaker. Their vision, creativity, and unselfishness are the hallmarks of their greatness. These players possess a rare combination of skill and intelligence that allows them to control the game and leave an indelible mark on hockey.

In conclusion, the playmakers are the game's architects, crafting unforgettable moments on the ice and inspiring generations of players to come. Their impact on the sport is immeasurable, and their legacy will continue to shape the future of hockey for years to come.

The Snipers: Scoring Machines on Ice

In the high-octane world of ice hockey, few players capture the imagination and admiration of fans like the snipers. These scoring machines possess an uncanny ability to find the back of the net, often in the most spectacular and unexpected ways. With lightning-fast reflexes, pinpoint accuracy, and nerves of steel, the snipers have etched their names in the annals of hockey history as some of the most prolific and exciting players ever to grace the ice.

The art of sniping in hockey is a delicate balance of skill, timing, and instinct. It requires exceptional hand-eye coordination and puck control, an innate understanding of the game's geometry, and the ability to read the opposition's movements. The best snipers in the sport's history have combined these attributes with a relentless work ethic and an insatiable hunger for goals.

One cannot discuss hockey snipers without mentioning the legendary Wayne Gretzky. Known as "The Great One," Gretzky is widely regarded as the greatest hockey player of all time. His incredible vision, creativity, and scoring touch allowed him to shatter numerous records, including the most goals in a single season (92) and the most career goals (894). Gretzky's ability to find open space on the ice and exploit even the tiniest defensive lapses made him a constant threat to opposing teams.

Another iconic sniper in hockey history is Maurice "Rocket" Richard. The first player to score 50 goals in a single season, Richard's powerful shot and explosive speed earned him his famous nickname. His fierce determination and passion for the game inspired generations of players and helped to establish the Montreal Canadiens as one of the most successful franchises in the sport.

Recently, snipers like Alexander Ovechkin and Steven Stamkos have continued to dazzle fans with their goal-scoring prowess. Ovechkin, known as "The Great Eight," has consistently been among the league's top goal-scorers since his debut in 2005. His size, strength, and skill combination have made him nearly unstoppable in the offensive zone. On the other hand, Stamkos is renowned for his lethal one-timer and ability to score from almost anywhere on the ice.

While the snipers may often steal the spotlight with their highlight-reel goals, their success is often the result of a collective effort from their teammates. The playmakers, who set up these scoring opportunities with their vision and passing abilities, play a crucial role in the sniper's success. Together, they form a formidable partnership that can strike fear into the hearts of opposing teams.

In conclusion, the snipers of ice hockey are a unique breed of player, capable of turning a game on its head with a single flick of their wrist. Their ability to score goals in the most challenging of circumstances has earned them a special place in the hearts of fans and a revered status among their peers. As the sport continues to evolve, there is no doubt that future generations of snipers will emerge, ready to etch their names alongside the game's legends.

The Enforcers: Hockey's Toughest Competitors

In the high-speed, hard-hitting world of ice hockey, the enforcers are the gladiators who command respect and fear from their opponents. These tough competitors are the backbone of their teams, providing physicality, intimidation, and protection for their teammates. They are the players willing to drop the gloves and engage in fisticuffs to defend their team's honor, and their presence on the ice is a crucial element of the game's strategy and culture. In this section, we will delve into the careers and contributions of some of the most legendary enforcers in hockey history.

One cannot discuss hockey enforcers without mentioning the name Bob Probert. Known as the "Bruise Brother" alongside his Detroit Red Wings teammate Joey Kocur, Probert was a force to be reckoned with during his 16-year NHL career. With a combination of size, strength, and skill, Probert was a feared fighter who could also contribute offensively. His 3,300 career penalty minutes rank him among the most penalized players in NHL history, but his 384 career points demonstrate his versatility.

Another iconic enforcer is Dave "The Hammer" Schultz, who played a pivotal role in the Philadelphia Flyers' back-to-back Stanley Cup championships in 1974 and 1975. Schultz was the epitome of the "Broad Street Bullies" era in Philadelphia, using his fists to intimidate opponents and create space for his skilled teammates. His single-season record of 472 penalty minutes still stands today, and his willingness to stand up for his teammates made him a beloved figure in Flyers history.

Tiger Williams, the NHL's all-time leader in penalty minutes with 3,966, was another enforcer who struck fear into the hearts of his opponents. Williams was known for his aggressive style of play and his iconic goal celebrations, where he would ride his stick like a horse after scoring. Despite his reputation as a tough guy, Williams was also a skilled player, scoring over 500 points in his career.

In recent years, enforcers like Georges Laraque, Tie Domi, and Derek Boogaard have carried the tradition of rugged, physical play in the NHL. These players were known for their fighting prowess and ability to change a game's momentum with a single bout. While the role of the enforcer has evolved, with a greater emphasis on skill and speed in today's game, the impact of these legendary competitors cannot be understated.

The enforcers of hockey history have left an indelible mark on the sport, shaping its culture and identity in a way few other players can. Their toughness, courage, and unwavering commitment to their teammates have earned them a special place in the annals of hockey lore. So as we continue to celebrate the game's greatest legends, let us not forget the ice warriors who fought for every inch of the rink and stood tall in the face of adversity.

The Captains: Leaders of Legendary Teams

In the high-stakes world of professional hockey, the role of the team captain is one of immense responsibility and influence. These exceptional individuals are gifted athletes and have the unique ability to inspire, motivate, and guide their teammates to victory. In this section, we will explore the stories of some of the most iconic captains in hockey history, whose leadership and dedication have left an indelible mark on the sport.

One cannot discuss legendary hockey captains without mentioning Wayne Gretzky, the undisputed "Great One" of the game. As the captain of the Edmonton Oilers and later the Los Angeles Kings, Gretzky's extraordinary skill and vision on the ice were matched only by his ability to bring out the best in his teammates. Under his leadership, the

Oilers won four Stanley Cup championships in just five years, solidifying their place as one of the most dominant teams in NHL history.

Another iconic captain is Mark Messier, who succeeded Gretzky as the Oilers' captain and led the team to another Stanley Cup victory in 1990. Known for his fierce competitiveness and unwavering determination, Messier's leadership extended beyond the Oilers, as he later captained the New York Rangers to their first championship in 54 years. His famous guarantee of a victory in Game 6 of the 1994 Eastern Conference Finals, followed by a hat trick performance, remains one of the most memorable moments in hockey history.

The list of legendary captains would be incomplete without mentioning Steve Yzerman, the long-time captain of the Detroit Red Wings. Yzerman's tenure as captain spanned two decades, during which he led the team to three Stanley Cup championships and became the embodiment of the Red Wings' winning culture. His selfless play and commitment to the team earned him the respect of teammates and opponents, making him one of the most admired figures in the sport.

In more recent years, Sidney Crosby has emerged as one of the most successful captains of his generation. As the leader of the Pittsburgh Penguins, Crosby has guided the team to three Stanley Cup championships, all while maintaining his status as one of the game's most dominant players. His ability to perform under pressure and relentless work ethic have made him a role model for aspiring hockey players worldwide.

Finally, we must acknowledge the contributions of trailblazing captains from outside the NHL, such as Hayley Wickenheiser, who captained the Canadian women's national team to multiple Olympic gold medals and World Championship titles. Wickenheiser's leadership and skill on the ice have earned her a place among the greatest hockey players of all time and helped elevate the profile of women's hockey on the global stage.

In conclusion, the captains highlighted in this section represent the pinnacle of leadership and excellence in hockey. Their ability to unite and inspire their teams on and off the ice has left a lasting legacy that will continue to shape the sport for generations. As we celebrate the achievements of these remarkable individuals, we are reminded of the power of teamwork, determination, and the pursuit of greatness in the face of adversity.

The Coaches: Visionaries Behind the Bench

The success of a hockey team is not solely determined by the talent and skill of its players. Behind every great team is a visionary coach who masterminds the strategies, motivates the players, and instills a winning mentality. In this section, we will delve into the lives and careers of some of the most legendary coaches in hockey history, who have left an indelible mark on the sport with their innovative tactics, exceptional leadership, and unwavering dedication to the game.

One cannot discuss hockey coaching legends without mentioning Scotty Bowman, the winningest coach in NHL history. Bowman's coaching career spanned over three decades with an astounding nine Stanley Cup championships under his belt and saw him lead the St. Louis Blues, Montreal Canadiens, Buffalo Sabres, Pittsburgh Penguins, and Detroit Red Wings to victory. Known for his adaptability and keen understanding of the game, Bowman's ability to bring out the best in his players and make crucial adjustments during high-pressure situations set him apart from his contemporaries.

Another iconic figure in hockey coaching is Herb Brooks, best known for leading the 1980 U.S. Olympic hockey team to a miraculous victory against the heavily favored Soviet Union in what is now known as the "Miracle on Ice." Brooks' innovative coaching style, which emphasized speed, agility, and teamwork, revolutionized how the game was played in North America. His relentless pursuit of excellence and ability to inspire his players to believe in themselves and their teammates made him a true legend of the sport.

Al Arbour, the mastermind behind the New York Islanders dynasty in the early 1980s, is another coach who left an indelible mark on the sport. With his calm demeanor and focus on strong defensive play, Arbour led the Islanders to four consecutive Stanley Cup championships from 1980 to 1983. His emphasis on discipline, hard work, and team unity helped mold a group of talented individuals into a cohesive and unstoppable force on the ice.

The list of legendary hockey coaches would only be complete by mentioning the contributions of women in the sport. Digit Murphy, one of the most successful coaches in women's hockey, has been a trailblazer for gender equality in the sport. With over 20 years of coaching experience, Murphy has led teams to numerous championships, including six Women's Beanpot titles and two Eastern College Athletic Conference (ECAC) championships. In addition, her passion for the game and commitment to empowering female athletes has made her a role model for aspiring coaches and players.

In conclusion, the visionary coaches highlighted in this section have achieved remarkable success in their careers and have shaped the game of hockey in profound ways. Their innovative strategies, exceptional leadership, and unwavering dedication to the sport have left a lasting legacy that inspires future generations of players and coaches. As we celebrate the achievements of these hockey legends, we are reminded of the crucial role that coaches play in the development and success of the sport and its athletes.

The International Stage: Hockey Legends Around the World

The world of hockey is not confined to the borders of North America. The sport has a rich history and a passionate following in countries across the globe. From the frozen lakes of Scandinavia to the bustling areas of Eastern Europe, hockey legends have emerged to leave their indelible mark on the game. In this section, we will explore the stories of these international icons, who have excelled in their domestic leagues and represented their countries with pride and distinction on the international stage.

The European hockey scene has produced some of history's most skilled and talented players. Sweden, Finland, Russia, and the Czech Republic are just a few countries that have given birth to hockey legends. These players have dazzled fans with incredible skill, speed, and finesse and have often been the driving force behind their national teams' success in international competitions.

One cannot discuss international hockey legends without mentioning the Russian "Red Machine." The Soviet Union's national team dominated the international hockey scene for decades, producing some of history's most talented and feared players. Names like Vladislav Tretiak, Valeri Kharlamov, and Viacheslav Fetisov are synonymous with the Soviet hockey dynasty, and their impact on the game is still felt today.

Scandinavia has also been a hotbed for hockey talent, with Sweden and Finland producing numerous game legends. Swedish icons like Borje Salming, Mats Sundin, and Nicklas Lidstrom have left an indelible mark on the sport. At the same time, Finnish legends like Teemu Selanne, Jari Kurri, and Saku Koivu have inspired a new generation of players from their homeland.

The Czech Republic and Slovakia, two countries with shared hockey history, have also produced their fair share of legends. The likes of Jaromir Jagr, Dominik Hasek, and Peter Stastny have excelled in their domestic leagues and have been instrumental in their national teams' successes on the international stage.

While North America has been the epicenter of the hockey world, the sport's growth and development in Asia cannot be ignored. Countries like Japan, South Korea, and China have made significant strides in recent years, producing players who have gone on to compete at the highest levels of the sport. As the game continues to expand globally, it is only a matter of time before we see more legends emerge from these burgeoning hockey markets.

In conclusion, the international stage has been graced by some of the most talented and iconic players in the history of hockey. These legends have left their mark on the game and inspired countless others to follow in their footsteps. As the sport continues to grow and evolve, there is no doubt that the list of hockey legends worldwide will only continue to expand, further enriching the tapestry of this incredible game.

The Enduring Legacy of Hockey's Greatest Players

As we reach the end of our journey through the annals of hockey history, it is essential to reflect on the enduring legacy of the game's greatest players. These Ice Warriors have left an indelible mark on the sport and inspired generations of fans and aspiring athletes alike. Their incredible feats on the ice, unwavering dedication to the game, and exemplary sportsmanship have all contributed to the rich tapestry of hockey's storied past.

The legends we have explored in this chapter have transcended the boundaries of their respective eras, leaving a lasting impact on the sport that continues to be felt today. From the early pioneers who laid the groundwork for modern hockey to the international stars who have brought the game to new heights, these players have all played a crucial role in shaping the sport we know and love.

One of the most significant aspects of these legends' legacies is how they have inspired future generations of players. Young athletes worldwide look up to these icons, aspiring to emulate their skill, determination, and passion for the game. In doing so, they carry on the traditions and values that have made hockey a beloved sport for over a century.

Moreover, the impact of these players extends beyond the ice. Many of them have used their fame and influence to give back to their communities, championing charitable causes and promoting the importance of sportsmanship, teamwork, and perseverance. In this way, they have become role models for aspiring hockey players and people from all walks of life.

As we celebrate the achievements of these extraordinary individuals, it is important to remember that their stories are not just about goals, assists, and championships. They are also about the human spirit, the drive to overcome adversity and the pursuit of excellence in the face of seemingly insurmountable odds. These are the qualities that define true legends, and they are the qualities that will continue to inspire future generations of hockey players and fans alike.

In conclusion, the enduring legacy of hockey's greatest players is a testament to the power of the sport to captivate, inspire, and unite people from all corners of the globe. As we look back on the incredible careers of these Ice Warriors, we are reminded of the timeless appeal of hockey and the countless ways in which it has enriched our lives. And as the game continues to evolve and grow, we can be confident that new legends will emerge, adding their unique chapters to the ever-expanding story of this great sport.

7

THE DIAMOND STARS: BASEBALL LEGENDS

Baseball Smash

Baseball, often called America's pastime, has captured the hearts and minds of millions of fans for well over a century. From the bat's crack to the crowd's roar, the game has produced countless unforgettable moments and legendary figures who have left an indelible mark on the sport's rich history. In this chapter, we will delve into the lives and careers of the diamond stars – the baseball legends who have transcended the game and become icons in their own right.

These extraordinary athletes have showcased their remarkable skills on the field and shaped the game in ways that continue to resonate with fans today. From the early pioneers who set the stage for baseball's golden age to the modern-day superstars who are redefining the sport, these legends represent baseball's very best.

As we journey through the annals of baseball history, we will explore the stories of the power hitters who captivated fans with their awe-inspiring home runs, the pitching phenoms who dominated the mound with their incredible arms, and the speed demons who dazzled with their lightning-fast base stealing and defensive magic. We will also pay tribute to the iron men whose record-breaking streaks and longevity in the game have become the stuff of legend and the barrier breakers who courageously paved the way for integration and inclusion in the sport.

In addition, we will recognize the contributions of the managers and coaches who masterminded the success of their teams, as well as the unsung heroes whose accomplishments may have been overlooked but are no less deserving of recognition. Finally, we will examine the legacy of these baseball legends and how their enduring impact continues to inspire future generations of players and fans alike.

As we embark on this journey through the lives and careers of baseball's all-time greats, we invite you to join us in celebrating the incredible achievements, unforgettable moments, and lasting legacies of the diamond stars who have forever etched their names in the annals of America's pastime.

The Early Pioneers: Setting the Stage for Baseball's Golden Age

As the sun began to rise on the world of professional baseball, a group of trailblazing athletes emerged, setting the stage for what would become America's favorite pastime. These early pioneers of the sport showcased their exceptional skills on the field and laid the groundwork for the generations of baseball legends that would follow in their footsteps. This section will delve into the lives and careers of these remarkable individuals who helped shape the game we know and love today.

The origins of baseball can be traced back to the mid-19th century, with the establishment of the National Association of Baseball Players in 1857. However, in the 1870s and 1880s, the sport truly began to capture the hearts and minds of the American public. This period saw the rise of several standout players who would become household names, such as Cap Anson, King Kelly, and Old Hoss Radbourn.

Cap Anson, born in 1852, was a versatile player who excelled both as a hitter and a fielder. Throughout his 27-year career, Anson amassed more than 3,000 hits and a lifetime batting average of .334, making him one of the most prolific hitters of his era. As the captain and manager of the Chicago White Stockings (later known as the Cubs), Anson led his team to five National League championships, solidifying his status as a true baseball legend.

Another early pioneer of the sport was King Kelly, a charismatic and flamboyant player who became one of the game's first superstars. Known for his daring base running and exceptional defensive skills, Kelly was a fan favorite and a key figure in popularizing baseball during the late 19th century. His larger-than-life personality and penchant for bending the rules earned him the nickname "The King of Baseball."

Old Hoss Radbourn, a dominant pitcher of the 1880s, was another trailblazer who left an indelible mark on the sport. In 1884, Radbourn set a record that still stands today, winning an astonishing 59 games in a single season. His incredible endurance and competitive spirit made him a force to be reckoned with on the mound, and his contributions to the game have not been forgotten.

These early pioneers were not only exceptional athletes but also instrumental in shaping the culture and spirit of baseball. They played with passion, grit, and determination, qualities that would define the sport in the future. Their influence extended beyond the field, as they helped to popularize the game and make it an integral part of American life.

As we continue our journey through the annals of baseball history, we will encounter many more legends who built upon the foundation laid by these early pioneers. From the power hitters and pitching phenoms to the barrier breakers and unsung heroes, these remarkable individuals played a crucial role in shaping the game we know and love today. But it all began with the trailblazing efforts of Cap Anson, King Kelly, Old Hoss Radbourn, and their contemporaries, who set the stage for baseball's golden age and the enduring legacy of America's pastime.

The Power Hitters: Home Run Kings Who Captivated Fans

In the storied history of baseball, few aspects of the game have captured the imagination and admiration of fans quite like the long ball. The crack of the bat, the soaring trajectory of the ball, and the eruption of cheers from the crowd as it clears the outfield fence – these moments have come to define the sport's most iconic power hitters. In this section, we will delve into the careers and achievements of the legendary sluggers who have left an indelible mark on the game with their awe-inspiring home runs.

One cannot discuss baseball's greatest power hitters without mentioning the Sultan of Swat, Babe Ruth. Ruth's larger-than-life persona and prodigious home run prowess revolutionized the sport in the 1920s and 1930s. With a career total of 714 home runs, Ruth held the record for decades and remains one of the most celebrated figures in baseball history.

Following Ruth's footsteps, Hank Aaron would surpass Babe's home run record in 1974, ultimately finishing his career with an astounding 755 home runs. Aaron's consistency, longevity at the plate, and quiet dignity and grace earned him the nickname "Hammerin' Hank" and the admiration of fans and fellow players alike.

Another iconic slugger who captivated fans with his tape-measure home runs was Mickey Mantle. The "Commerce Comet" spent his entire 18-year career with the New York Yankees, amassing 536 home runs and earning a reputation as one of the most feared hitters of his era. Mantle's prodigious power from both sides of the plate and his ability to hit for both average and power made him a true offensive force.

In more recent times, the 1990s and early 2000s saw the emergence of a new generation of power hitters, headlined by Ken Griffey Jr., Sammy Sosa, and Mark McGwire. Griffey's smooth swing and effortless power earned him 630 career home runs and a place among the game's all-time greats. Meanwhile, Sosa and McGwire's thrilling home run race in 1998 captivated the nation. Both players shattered Roger Maris's single-season record of 61 home runs, with McGwire ultimately finishing the season with an astonishing 70.

The modern era has also seen the rise of prolific power hitters such as Barry Bonds, who broke Hank Aaron's career home run record in 2007, finishing with a staggering 762 home runs. While allegations of performance-enhancing drug use have marred Bonds's achievements, there is no denying his impact on the game during his career.

These legendary power hitters have not only etched their names in the record books but have also left an indelible mark on the hearts and minds of baseball fans. Their towering home runs and unforgettable moments at the plate have become the stuff of legend, inspiring countless young players to dream of one day launching their majestic blasts into the stands. As the game continues to evolve, there is no doubt that future generations of power hitters will emerge, adding their own chapters to the rich history of baseball's home run kings.

The Pitching Phenoms: Dominant Arms on the Mound

Baseball, often called America's pastime, has been graced by numerous talented players throughout history. Among these gifted athletes, pitchers are some of the most captivating and awe-inspiring performers. With their incredible skill and mastery of the art of hurling a baseball, these pitching phenoms have left an indelible mark on the sport. This section will delve into the careers of some of the most dominant arms on the mound, whose exploits have earned them a place among baseball's greatest legends.

One cannot discuss the greatest pitchers in baseball history without mentioning the legendary Cy Young. With a career spanning over two decades, Young's incredible 511 wins remain an unbroken record to this day. His remarkable consistency and durability on the mound set the standard for future generations of pitchers. The prestigious Cy Young Award, given annually to the best pitcher in each league, is a testament to his enduring impact on the sport.

Another iconic figure in the world of pitching is the great Walter Johnson. Known as "The Big Train," Johnson's powerful fastball was a force to be reckoned with during his 21-year career. With 3,508 strikeouts and 110 shutouts to his name, Johnson's prowess on the mound earned him a place in the inaugural class of the Baseball Hall of Fame in 1936.

The name Sandy Koufax is synonymous with pitching excellence. Despite a relatively short career due to injury, Koufax's impact on the game is undeniable. With four no-hitters, including a perfect game, and three Cy Young Awards in just 12 seasons, Koufax's dominance on the mound remains a benchmark for greatness in baseball.

More recently, Greg Maddux, Randy Johnson, and Pedro Martinez have continued the tradition of pitching excellence. Maddux, known for his pinpoint control and ability to outsmart hitters, amassed an impressive 355 wins and four consecutive Cy Young Awards. Johnson, a towering figure at 6'10", used his intimidating presence and blazing fastball to strike fear into the hearts of opposing batters, racking up 4,875 strikeouts and five Cy Young Awards. Martinez, a smaller but equally dominant force on the mound, dazzled fans with his electric stuff and fiery competitiveness, earning three Cy Young Awards and a reputation as one of the most feared pitchers of his era.

With their unique blend of skill, determination, and artistry, these pitching phenoms have left an indelible mark on baseball. Their exploits on the mound have inspired countless young players to pick up a baseball and dream of one day emulating their heroes. As we continue to marvel at the incredible feats of today's pitching stars, we are reminded of the rich history of dominant arms that have graced the mound, forever etching their names in the annals of baseball lore.

The Speed Demons: Base Stealers and Defensive Wizards

In baseball, power, and strength often steal the spotlight, with home runs and strikeouts dominating the headlines. However, the true essence of the sport lies in the intricate details and the subtle skills that can make all the difference in a game. Among these skills, speed, and agility stand out as crucial elements that have shaped the careers of many baseball legends. In this section, we will delve into the world of the speed demons and defensive wizards who have left an indelible mark on the game with their lightning-fast reflexes and unparalleled athleticism.

Baseball has always been a game of strategy and timing, and few players have exemplified this better than the great base stealers of the sport. These athletes have an uncanny ability to read the pitcher's movements, anticipate the ball's trajectory, and make split-second decisions that often result in game-changing stolen bases. One such legend is Rickey Henderson, widely regarded as the greatest base stealer ever. With a record-breaking 1,406 stolen bases throughout his career, Henderson's speed and instincts on the basepaths were extraordinary.

Another speed demon who made a name for himself with his base-stealing prowess was Lou Brock. Brock held the record with 938 career stolen bases before Henderson surpassed him. His incredible speed and quickness made him a threat on the basepaths and contributed to his success as an outfielder, where he was known for his impressive range and ability to chase down fly balls.

While base stealers often garner much of the attention when it comes to speed in baseball, defensive wizards in the field have also played a significant role in shaping the sport's history. Ozzie Smith, nicknamed "The Wizard," was a master of the shortstop position, dazzling fans and opponents alike with his acrobatic plays and seemingly impossible catches. Smith's defensive prowess earned him 13 Gold Glove Awards and a place in the hearts of baseball fans everywhere.

Another defensive legend who significantly impacted the game was Brooks Robinson. Known as the "Human Vacuum Cleaner," Robinson's extraordinary reflexes and agility at third base made him one of the best defensive players in the sport's history. His ability to make difficult plays look routine earned him 16 consecutive Gold Glove Awards and a reputation as one of the most reliable players in the game.

In the modern era, players like Ichiro Suzuki and Andrelton Simmons have continued the legacy of speed and defensive excellence in baseball. With his lightning-fast speed and incredible arm strength, Ichiro has become one of the most respected outfielders in the game, while Simmons' jaw-dropping plays at shortstop have earned him comparisons to the great Ozzie Smith.

The impact of these speed demons and defensive wizards on baseball cannot be overstated. Their extraordinary skills have led to individual success and contributed to their teams' success, often turning the tide in crucial moments and making the difference between victory and defeat. So, as we continue to marvel at the power and strength displayed by today's baseball stars, let us not forget the speed and agility that have shaped the careers of these legendary athletes and forever changed the way we view the sport.

The Iron Men: Record-Breaking Streaks and Longevity in the Game

In baseball's storied history, some players have demonstrated exceptional skill and talent and an unwavering dedication to the game. These "Iron Men" of baseball have defied the odds, pushing their bodies and minds to the limit in pursuit of greatness. Their record-breaking streaks and longevity in the game have left an indelible mark on the sport, inspiring generations of players and fans alike.

One of the most iconic Iron Men in baseball history is Lou

Gehrig. Known as the "Iron Horse," Gehrig played for the New York Yankees from 1923 to 1939. His incredible streak of 2,130 consecutive games played stood as a record for 56 years until it was broken by Cal Ripken Jr. in 1995. Gehrig's remarkable durability and consistency were matched only by his prowess at the plate, as he finished his career with a .340 batting average, 493 home runs, and 1,995 runs batted in.

Cal Ripken Jr., who surpassed Gehrig's consecutive games played record, is another shining example of an Iron Man in baseball. Ripken's streak of 2,632 games played is a testament to his incredible work ethic and commitment to the game. Over his 21-year career with the Baltimore Orioles, Ripken earned the nickname "The Iron Man" and became one of the most beloved players in the sport. His impressive career statistics include 3,184 hits, 431 home runs, and 19 All-Star Game appearances.

Nolan Ryan, one of the most dominant pitchers in baseball history, also exemplifies the Iron Man spirit. Over an astounding 27-year career, Ryan struck fear into the hearts of opposing batters with his blazing fastball and devastating curveball. Ryan's longevity in the game is nothing short of remarkable, as he pitched until the age of 46. His career achievements include a record 5,714 strikeouts, seven no-hitters, and eight All-Star Game selections.

Another Iron Man worth mentioning is Pete Rose, who holds the record for most career hits with 4,256. Rose's relentless pursuit of excellence and unmatched passion for the game allowed him to play for 24 seasons, earning him the nickname "Charlie Hustle." Despite the controversy surrounding his later years, Rose's on-field accomplishments and longevity remain a testament to his dedication and love for baseball.

These Iron Men of Baseball have shown that with hard work, determination, and an unwavering commitment to the game, it can achieve greatness and leave a lasting legacy. Their record-breaking streaks and longevity in the game serve as a reminder that the human spirit can triumph over adversity and that the pursuit of excellence is a worthy endeavor. As future generations of baseball players take the field, they will look to these legends for inspiration and strive to emulate their Iron Man spirit.

The Barrier Breakers: Pioneers of Integration and Inclusion

Baseball, like any other sport, has been a reflection of society's progress and evolution. Throughout history, the game has seen numerous trailblazers who have broken barriers and paved the way for a more inclusive and diverse sport. These barrier breakers have not only changed the face of baseball but have also played a significant role in promoting social change and equality.

One of the most iconic figures in this regard is Jackie Robinson. In 1947, Robinson shattered the color barrier in Major League Baseball when he debuted for the Brooklyn Dodgers. As the first African American to play in the major leagues in the modern era, Robinson faced immense racism and hostility both on and off the field. Despite these challenges, he persevered and excelled, earning the Rookie of the Year award in his first season and eventually being inducted into the Baseball Hall of Fame. Robinson's courage and determination opened the door for countless other African American players, forever changing the landscape of the sport.

Another trailblazer in baseball was Roberto Clemente, the first Latin American and Caribbean player to be inducted into the Hall of Fame. Hailing from Puerto Rico, Clemente faced language barriers and cultural differences when he began his career with the Pittsburgh Pirates in 1955. Despite these obstacles, he became one of the most beloved and respected players in the game, known for his exceptional skills and humanitarian efforts off the field. Clemente's success helped pave the way for the influx of Latin American talent that has since become an integral part of baseball's identity.

In more recent years, baseball has seen the rise of players from Asia, further diversifying the sport and breaking down barriers. Ichiro Suzuki, a Japanese outfielder, made history in 2001 when he joined the Seattle Mariners and became the first-position player from Japan to play in the major leagues. Ichiro's success, including winning both the

Rookie of the Year and Most Valuable Player awards in his first season, opened the door for other Asian players to make their mark in the major leagues.

The fight for inclusion in baseball has not been limited to players from different racial and ethnic backgrounds. In 2015, Justine Siegal became the first woman to coach in Major League Baseball when the Oakland Athletics hired her as a guest instructor for their instructional league team. Siegal's groundbreaking achievement has helped pave the way for other women to pursue baseball careers on and off the field.

The barrier breakers in baseball have played a crucial role in promoting diversity and inclusion within the sport. Their courage, determination, and talent have changed the game and inspired countless individuals from all walks of life to pursue their dreams, regardless of the obstacles they may face. As baseball continues to evolve and grow, the legacy of these pioneers will undoubtedly live on, reminding us of the power of sport to unite and uplift.

The Managers and Coaches: Masterminds Behind the Success

In baseball, the spotlight often shines on the players who hit towering home runs, make dazzling defensive plays, or throw blazing fastballs. However, behind every successful team lies a brilliant mind orchestrating the game from the dugout. Managers and coaches are the unsung heroes of baseball, responsible for crafting strategies, developing talent, and fostering team chemistry. In this section, we will delve into the lives and careers of baseball's most influential and successful managers and coaches.

One cannot discuss baseball's greatest managers without mentioning the legendary Connie Mack. With a managerial career spanning 53 years, Mack led the Philadelphia Athletics to five World Series titles and accumulated over 3,700 wins. Known for his calm demeanor and strategic acumen, Mack was a master at getting the most out of his players and adapting to the ever-changing landscape of the sport.

Another titan of the dugout is the fiery and passionate Tommy

Lasorda. As the Los Angeles Dodgers manager for 20 years, Lasorda guided the team to two World Series championships and four National League pennants. His ability to motivate and inspire his players was unmatched and his love for the game was infectious. In addition, Lasorda's larger-than-life personality made him a beloved figure in Los Angeles and throughout the baseball world.

In recent times, the name Joe Torre has become synonymous with managerial success. As the skipper of the New York Yankees from 1996 to 2007, Torre led the team to four World Series titles and six American League pennants. His calm and steady presence in the dugout was a perfect fit for the high-pressure environment of New York, and his ability to manage the egos of a star-studded roster was instrumental in the Yankees' dominance during his tenure.

The role of a coach in baseball cannot be underestimated, as they are responsible for developing and refining players' skills at every level. One of the most influential coaches in history is the renowned pitching guru Leo Mazzone. As the pitching coach for the Atlanta Braves from 1990 to 2005, Mazzone was the architect behind one of the most dominant pitching staffs in baseball history, featuring Hall of Famers Greg Maddux, Tom Glavine, and John Smoltz. Mazzone's innovative techniques and relentless work ethic revolutionized how pitchers were coached and helped the Braves achieve unparalleled success on the mound.

In conclusion, the impact of managers and coaches on the success of a baseball team cannot be overstated. These game masterminds have shaped countless legends' careers and left an indelible mark on the sport. Their strategic prowess, ability to develop talent, and unwavering dedication to the game have earned them a place among baseball's greatest legends. So, as we continue to marvel at the feats of today's baseball stars, let us remember the brilliant minds guiding them from the dugout.

The Unsung Heroes: Overlooked Legends Who Made Their Mark

In baseball's storied history, countless legends have left an indelible mark on the game. While many of these players are household names, there are others who, despite their immense talent and contributions, have not received the recognition they deserve. These unsung heroes have played pivotal roles in shaping the sport, and their stories deserve to be told.

One overlooked legend is Minnie Miñoso, a Cuban-born outfielder who played in the Major Leagues from 1949 to 1980. Known as the "Cuban Comet," Miñoso was a trailblazer for Latino players in the United States. He was the first black Cuban player in the Major Leagues and the first black player for the Chicago White Sox. A nine-time All-Star, Miñoso was a dynamic player who excelled in all aspects of the game, from hitting for power and average to fielding and base running. Yet, despite his impressive career, Miñoso must be inducted into the Baseball Hall of Fame, a fact many fans and experts consider a glaring oversight.

Another unsung hero is Larry Doby, the second African American player to break the color barrier in Major League Baseball, just months after Jackie Robinson. Doby's debut with the Cleveland Indians in 1947 marked the beginning of racial integration in the American League. A seven-time All-Star, Doby was a powerful hitter and an excellent outfielder, helping lead the Indians to a World Series championship in 1948. While Robinson's groundbreaking achievements are rightfully celebrated, Doby's contributions to the integration of baseball are often overshadowed.

In the realm of pitching, one cannot overlook the accomplishments of Luis Tiant. Born in Cuba, Tiant was a dominant force on the mound during his 19-year career in the Major Leagues. Known for his unorthodox windup and devastating curveball, Tiant was a three-time All-Star and led the American League twice in earned run average (ERA). Despite his impressive statistics and memorable performances, Tiant still needs to be enshrined in the Baseball Hall of Fame.

The world of baseball would only be complete with acknowledging the contributions of women who have made their mark on the sport. Toni Stone, Mamie "Peanut" Johnson, and Connie Morgan were three talented women who played in the Negro Leagues during the 1950s. These trailblazing women faced significant challenges and discrimination, but their skill and determination paved the way for future generations of female athletes.

Finally, the story of unsung heroes in baseball would not be complete without mentioning the countless players from the Negro Leagues who never had the opportunity to showcase their talents in the Major Leagues due to the color barrier. Stars like Josh Gibson, Oscar Charleston, and Cool Papa Bell were among the greatest players of their time, and their impact on the game should never be forgotten.

In conclusion, the unsung heroes of baseball have made significant contributions to the sport, both on and off the field. Their stories serve as a reminder that greatness can be found in unexpected places and that the true measure of a legend is not always found in the record books or the Hall of Fame but in the hearts and minds of those who love the game.

The Modern Era: Baseball Stars Shining Bright in the 21st Century

As the sun sets on the golden age of baseball, a new generation of stars has risen to carry the torch of America's pastime into the 21st century. These modern-day legends have dazzled fans with their incredible skills and athleticism and redefined the game in ways that their predecessors could have never imagined. In this section, we will explore the careers of some of the most iconic baseball players of the modern era, who have left an indelible mark on the sport and continue to inspire future generations of athletes.

The 21st century has seen the emergence of several outstanding hitters who have captivated fans with their power and precision at the plate. Among them is Albert Pujols, a Dominican-born slugger who has consistently ranked among the game's elite since making his Major League debut in 2001. With over 600 home runs and counting, Pujols has etched his name in the annals of baseball history as one of the greatest power hitters ever.

Another modern-day hitting sensation is Miguel Cabrera, a Venezuelan-born player who has earned a reputation as one of the most feared hitters in the game. Cabrera's remarkable consistency and ability to hit for both power and average have earned him numerous accolades, including two American League MVP awards and the prestigious Triple Crown in 2012.

On the pitching front, the 21st century has been graced by several dominant arms, such as Clayton Kershaw and Justin Verlander. Kershaw, a left-handed pitcher known for his devastating curveball, has been a perennial Cy Young Award contender since his debut in 2008. With multiple no-hitters and a World Series title under his belt, Kershaw has solidified his status as one of the greatest pitchers of his generation.

On the other hand, Verlander has been a model of consistency and durability throughout his career. The hard-throwing right-hander has amassed over 3,000 strikeouts and has contributed to multiple championship-winning teams, including the 2017 Houston Astros.

The modern era has also witnessed the rise of several speed demons and defensive wizards, such as Ichiro Suzuki and Andrelton Simmons. Ichiro, a Japanese-born outfielder, took the baseball world by storm in 2001 with his unique blend of speed, contact hitting, and exceptional defense. With over 3,000 hits in the Major Leagues and numerous Gold Glove awards, Ichiro has left an indelible mark on the game and inspired countless young players worldwide.

Simmons, a shortstop from Curaçao, has dazzled fans with his acrobatic defense and incredible range. Widely regarded as one of the best defensive players in the game, Simmons has earned multiple Gold Glove awards and has consistently ranked among the league leaders in defensive metrics.

As we look back on the careers of these modern-day baseball legends, it is clear that their impact on the game will be felt for generations to come. Their remarkable achievements have redefined the sport and served as a testament to the enduring appeal of baseball in the 21st century. As the game continues to evolve, there is no doubt that these stars will continue to shine brightly, inspiring future generations of athletes to chase their dreams and etch their names in the annals of baseball history.

The Legacy: How Baseball Legends Continue to Inspire Future Generations

The impact of baseball legends on the sport and society cannot be overstated. These extraordinary athletes have not only left their mark on the record books but have also inspired countless individuals to pursue their dreams, both on and off the field. The legacy of these legends continues to shape the future of baseball, as new generations of players and fans look up to them as role models and strive to emulate their success.

One of the most significant ways baseball legends inspire future generations is through their dedication to the game. These athletes' hard work, perseverance, and commitment serve as a blueprint for aspiring players. Young athletes learn the importance of discipline, teamwork, and sportsmanship from the examples set by their heroes. The stories of legends overcoming adversity, such as Jackie Robinson breaking the color barrier or Lou Gehrig's battle with ALS, teach valuable life lessons about resilience and courage.

Another aspect of the legacy left by baseball legends is the way they have expanded the sport's reach and popularity. Players like Babe Ruth, Mickey Mantle, and Joe DiMaggio captured fans' imagination and helped establish baseball as America's pastime. In addition, their larger-than-life personas transcended the sport, making them household names and cultural icons. Modern stars like Mike Trout, Mookie Betts, and Shohei Ohtani continue to draw new fans to the game, ensuring its continued growth and success.

Baseball legends have also played a crucial role in breaking down barriers and promoting inclusivity within the sport. Pioneers like Jackie Robinson, Roberto Clemente, and Ichiro Suzuki paved the way for players of diverse backgrounds to excel at the highest level. Their achievements have inspired countless young athletes from underrepresented communities to pursue their dreams in baseball and beyond. The impact of these trailblazers can be seen in the increasingly diverse makeup of Major League Baseball, as well as in the global popularity of the sport.

The influence of baseball legends extends beyond the playing field, as many have used their fame and success to make a difference in their communities. Philanthropy and activism have become integral parts of the legacy left by these athletes. From Roberto Clemente's humanitarian efforts to Derek Jeter's Turn 2 Foundation, baseball legends have demonstrated the importance of giving back and using their platform to create positive change.

In conclusion, the enduring impact of baseball's greatest legends can be seen in how they inspire future generations of players and fans. Their dedication to the game, trailblazing efforts in breaking down barriers, and commitment to making a difference off the field have left an indelible mark on the sport and society. As new stars rise and records are broken, the legacy of these legends will live on, ensuring that the rich history and tradition of baseball continue to captivate and inspire for years to come.

The Enduring Impact of Baseball's Greatest Legends

As we reach the end of our journey through the annals of baseball history, it is essential to reflect on the enduring impact of the game's greatest legends. These remarkable athletes, managers, and pioneers have left an indelible mark on the sport, transcending the boundaries of the baseball diamond and influencing generations of fans and players alike.

The stories of these legends serve as a testament to the power of perseverance, hard work, and dedication. They have overcome adversity, shattered records, and defied expectations, all while captivating the hearts and minds of millions. Their achievements have not only shaped the game of baseball but have also become an integral part of American culture and history.

The sport's early pioneers laid the foundation for the game we know and love today. They set the stage for baseball's golden age, paving the way for future legends to make their mark. The power hitters, pitching phenoms, and speed demons dazzled fans with their extraordinary skills and athleticism, while the Iron Man demonstrated the importance of consistency and longevity in the game.

The barrier breakers, such as Jackie Robinson and Roberto Clemente, were crucial in promoting integration and inclusion in baseball. Their courage and resilience in the face of adversity have inspired countless individuals to pursue their dreams, regardless of their obstacles. With their strategic acumen and leadership, the managers and coaches have guided their teams to victory and shaped the careers of many legendary players.

The unsung heroes, though often overlooked, have made significant contributions to the sport, leaving a lasting impact on the game and its fans. The modern era of baseball has seen the rise of new stars who continue to push the boundaries of what is possible on the field, thrilling fans and setting new benchmarks for future generations to aspire to.

The legacy of baseball's greatest legends is not limited to their on-field accomplishments. Their stories of triumph and adversity have inspired countless individuals, both within and outside the realm of sports. In addition, they have taught us valuable lessons about the importance of determination, teamwork, and sportsmanship and shown us that anything is possible with passion and commitment.

In conclusion, baseball's greatest legends' enduring impact is evident in how they have shaped the game, inspired future generations, and left an indelible mark on our collective consciousness. As we continue to celebrate their achievements and remember their contributions, we are reminded of the magic and allure of America's pastime. These legends have not only enriched the sport of baseball but have also become an integral part of the tapestry of our lives, leaving a legacy that will undoubtedly endure for generations to come.

8

THE RACQUET MASTERS: TENNIS LEGENDS

Tennis Player in Action

Tennis, a sport that has captivated the hearts and minds of millions worldwide, is a game of skill, strategy, and endurance. This sport has produced some of the most iconic and memorable moments in athletics history. From the grass courts of Wimbledon to the clay courts of Roland Garros, tennis has been a stage for extraordinary athletes to showcase their talent, determination, and passion for the game. In this chapter, we will delve into the lives and careers of the greatest tennis legends who have graced the sport with their presence, leaving an indelible mark on its history.

The game of tennis has evolved significantly since its inception in the 12th century when it was played with bare hands and a ball made of leather. Over the centuries, the sport has transformed into a global phenomenon, with players wielding state-of-the-art racquets and competing in prestigious tournaments across the globe. The sport's rich history is filled with remarkable athletes who have pushed the boundaries of what was thought possible on the tennis court, inspiring generations of fans and players alike.

In this chapter, we will journey through the different tennis eras, highlighting the legends who have left an indelible mark on the sport. We will begin with the early 20th century, exploring the careers of tennis pioneers who laid the foundation for the modern game. Then, as we move through the decades, we will discuss the icons who defined the swinging sixties, the trailblazing female players who fought for gender equality in the sport, and the epic rivalries that captivated fans worldwide.

We will also delve into the careers of the modern masters who have dominated the sport in the 21st century, breaking records and redefining the limits of athletic achievement. Along the way, we will pay tribute to the style icons who have transformed the sport's fashion, the inspirational stories of players who have overcome adversity, and the up-and-coming stars who represent the future of tennis.

Finally, we will reflect on the legacy of these tennis legends, examining how their contributions have shaped the sport and influenced the generations of players who have followed in their footsteps. Through their talent, dedication, and passion for the game, these extraordinary athletes have left an enduring impact on the world of tennis, inspiring fans and players alike to strive for greatness both on and off the court.

The Golden Era: Tennis Legends of the Early 20th Century

As the sun began to set in the 19th century, a new dawn emerged for tennis. The early 20th century marked the beginning of what many consider the Golden Era of tennis when the sport's greatest legends graced the courts and left an indelible mark on the game. This chapter will delve into the lives and careers of these extraordinary athletes who set the stage for the modern game we know and love today.

The early 1900s saw the rise of tennis as a popular sport, with the establishment of prestigious tournaments such as Wimbledon, the French Open, and the US Open. During this time, the first true tennis legends emerged, captivating audiences with their exceptional skills, fierce determination, and unparalleled sportsmanship.

One of the most iconic figures of this era was Bill Tilden, an American tennis player who dominated the sport in the 1920s. Tilden's powerful serve and volley game, combined with his tactical brilliance, earned him ten Grand Slam titles and a place in the International Tennis Hall of Fame. His rivalry with French player René Lacoste, one of the famous "Four Musketeers" of French tennis, was the stuff of legend, with their matches drawing massive crowds and generating intense media interest.

Another standout player of this era was Suzanne Lenglen, a French tennis star who revolutionized the women's game. Lenglen's aggressive playing style and flamboyant on-court fashion made her a fan favorite and a symbol of the changing times. She won 31 Grand Slam titles, including six Wimbledon singles championships, and her rivalry with American player Helen Wills Moody was one of the most storied in tennis history.

The Golden Era also saw the rise of Australian tennis legends such as Norman Brookes, the first non-British player to win Wimbledon, and Gerald Patterson, a two-time Wimbledon champion. These players, along with others like Anthony Wilding of New Zealand and Henri Cochet of France, helped establish tennis as a truly international sport, paving the way for future generations of players worldwide.

As the Golden Era progressed, tennis continued evolving on and off the court. Introducing new racket technology, such as the steel-framed racket, allowed players to generate more power and spin. At the same time, adopting a standardized scoring system made the game more accessible to fans. The sport also began to attract a more diverse range of players, with trailblazers like Althea Gibson breaking down racial barriers and inspiring countless others to follow in her footsteps.

In conclusion, the Golden Era of tennis was a time of great innovation and excitement, as the sport's earliest legends pushed the boundaries of what was possible on the court. Their remarkable achievements, individually and collectively, laid the foundation for the modern game and continue to inspire tennis players and fans worldwide. As we move through the chapters of this book, we will see how the legacy of these early 20th-century tennis legends has been carried forward by subsequent generations of players, each adding their unique contributions to the rich tapestry of tennis history.

The Swinging Sixties: Tennis Icons Who Defined the Decade

The 1960s was a decade of significant change, both on and off the tennis court. As the world underwent a cultural revolution, tennis experienced a transformation, with a new generation of players emerging to challenge the established order. These icons dominated the sport during this era and left an indelible mark on the game, inspiring future generations of players and fans alike. In this section, we will explore the lives and careers of some of the most influential tennis legends of the Swinging Sixties.

Australian legend Rod Laver was one of the most iconic figures of this era. Known as "The Rocket" for his explosive playing style, Laver was the first player to win the Grand Slam (all four major championships in a single calendar year) twice, achieving this remarkable feat in 1962 and 1969. His aggressive serve-and-volley game, exceptional speed, and agility made him a formidable opponent on all surfaces. Laver's 200 career titles, including 11 Grand Slam singles titles, remain a testament to his extraordinary talent and dedication to the sport.

Another prominent figure of the 1960s was American tennis star Arthur Ashe. Ashe made history in 1968 when he became the first African American man to win a Grand Slam title, triumphing at the US Open. A powerful server and tactically astute player, Ashe's career highlights include three Grand Slam singles titles and a successful stint as the US Davis Cup team captain. Off the court, Ashe was a tireless advocate for civil rights and social justice, using his platform to raise awareness about racial inequality and the importance of education.

The Swinging Sixties also saw the rise of female tennis legends who would go on to redefine the women's game. Billie Jean King, one of the most influential figures in tennis history, was a dominant force during this decade. With 39 Grand Slam titles, including 12 in singles, King was a trailblazer both on and off the court. Her victory over Bobby Riggs in the famous "Battle of the Sexes" match in 1973 was pivotal in the fight for gender equality in sports. King's advocacy for equal pay and opportunities for female athletes has impacted tennis and beyond.

Another female tennis icon of the 1960s was Brazilian player Maria Bueno. Known for her elegant playing style and graceful demeanor, Bueno won 19 Grand Slam titles, including seven in singles. Her rivalry with fellow legend Margaret Court captivated tennis fans throughout the decade as the two players battled for supremacy on the world stage. Bueno's success helped to popularize tennis in her home country and paved the way for future generations of Brazilian tennis stars.

In conclusion, the Swinging Sixties was a decade that witnessed the rise of some of the most iconic and influential tennis legends in the sport's history. These players achieved remarkable success on the court and played a crucial role in shaping the cultural and social landscape of the era. Their enduring legacies continue to inspire and captivate tennis fans worldwide as the sport evolves and grows.

The Battle of the Sexes: Pioneering Female Tennis Legends

The world of tennis has been graced by numerous female players who have not only displayed exceptional talent on the court but have also broken barriers and paved the way for future generations. These pioneering women have challenged societal norms, fought for equal opportunities, and inspired countless others with their resilience and determination. In this section, we will delve into the lives and careers of some of the most influential female tennis legends who have left an indelible mark on the sport.

Billie Jean King: The Trailblazer

Billie Jean King is undoubtedly one of the most iconic figures in tennis history. With 39 Grand Slam titles to her name, King's prowess on the court is unquestionable. However, her impact extends far beyond her athletic achievements. As a staunch advocate for gender equality, King played a pivotal role in establishing the Women's Tennis Association (WTA) and introducing equal prize money for men and women at the US Open.

Perhaps her most famous moment came in 1973 when she defeated Bobby Riggs in the "Battle of the Sexes" match, a landmark event that garnered widespread attention and helped to change public perception of women's tennis. King's unwavering commitment to social justice and trailblazing efforts have left a lasting legacy in tennis.

Martina Navratilova: The Fearless Champion

Martina Navratilova's illustrious career boasts an astounding 59 Grand Slam titles, making her one of the most successful tennis players ever. Navratilova's aggressive playing style and exceptional athleticism revolutionized the women's game, inspiring a new generation of powerful and athletic players.

Off the court, Navratilova has been a fearless advocate for LGBTQ+ rights and has used her platform to raise awareness about various social issues. As one of the first openly gay athletes, Navratilova's courage and outspokenness have helped to break down barriers and challenge stereotypes, making her a true pioneer in the world of sports.

Serena Williams: The Modern Icon

Serena Williams is a name synonymous with greatness. With 23 Grand Slam singles titles and counting, Williams has become one of the greatest tennis players ever. Her powerful serve, relentless work ethic, and unmatched mental toughness have made her a force to be reckoned with on the court.

Williams' impact, however, extends beyond her athletic achievements. As a woman of color in a predominantly white sport, Williams has faced numerous challenges and prejudices throughout her career. Despite these obstacles, she has continued to excel and has used her platform to advocate for racial and gender equality. Williams' success and influence have inspired countless young girls, particularly those from underrepresented backgrounds, to pursue their dreams in the world of sports.

The Doubles Duos: Venus Williams and Serena Williams, Martina Navratilova and Pam Shriver

The tennis world has also witnessed some great female doubles partnerships that have left an indelible mark on the sport. With their powerful serves and exceptional athleticism, Venus and Serena Williams have dominated the doubles circuit, winning 14 Grand Slam titles together. In addition, their sisterly bond and mutual support have endeared them to fans worldwide.

Similarly, the partnership of Martina Navratilova and Pam Shriver was nothing short of legendary. With 21 Grand Slam doubles titles, the duo's fantastic chemistry and complementary playing styles made them a formidable force on the court.

In conclusion, the pioneering female tennis legends discussed in this section have displayed exceptional talent and skill on the court and have used their platforms to challenge societal norms, advocate for equality, and inspire future generations. Their enduring impact on tennis is a testament to their resilience, determination, and passion.

The Rivalries: Epic Clashes Between Tennis Titans

Throughout tennis history, rivalries have played a crucial role in shaping the sport and capturing the imaginations of fans worldwide. These epic clashes between tennis titans have showcased the highest level of skill and athleticism and the players' mental fortitude and unwavering determination. This section will delve into some of the most iconic rivalries that have left an indelible mark on tennis.

One of the earliest and most celebrated rivalries in tennis history was between American legends Bill Tilden and Bill Johnston. Their fierce battles in the 1920s captivated audiences and helped popularize the sport in the United States. Tilden, known for his powerful serve and tactical prowess, faced off against Johnston, a master of the forehand and a formidable opponent, in numerous championship matches. Their rivalry elevated the level of play and set the stage for future generations of tennis stars.

The 1970s and 1980s saw the emergence of several iconic rivalries, including the unforgettable battles between Bjorn Borg and John McEnroe. Their contrasting styles of play and personalities – Borg's ice-cold demeanor and relentless baseline game versus McEnroe's fiery temperament and serve-and-volley tactics – made for thrilling encounters on the court. Their most famous match, the 1980 Wimbledon final, is still regarded as one of the greatest tennis matches ever.

Another legendary rivalry from this era was between Chris Evert and Martina Navratilova. These two extraordinary athletes faced each other an astounding 80 times, with Navratilova holding a slight edge in their head-to-head record. Their matches were characterized by Evert's relentless consistency and Navratilova's aggressive net play, making for a fascinating contrast in styles. Their rivalry pushed each other to new heights and inspired a generation of female tennis players.

In more recent times, the tennis world has been enthralled by the epic battles between Roger Federer, Rafael Nadal, and Novak Djokovic – the "Big Three" of men's tennis. Their intense rivalries have produced some of the most memorable matches in tennis history, with each player pushing the others to evolve and improve their games constantly. Federer's elegant shot-making, Nadal's ferocious intensity, and Djokovic's unparalleled consistency have created a golden era of men's tennis that has captivated fans for nearly two decades.

On the women's side, the rivalry between Serena Williams and Venus Williams has been a defining feature of the sport since the late 1990s. The sisters have faced each other in numerous Grand Slam finals, with Serena often coming out on top. Their powerful serves, aggressive baseline play, and unyielding determination have made for thrilling matches and paved the way for a new generation of powerful and athletic female players.

These epic rivalries have provided tennis fans with countless unforgettable moments and played a crucial role in shaping the sport's history. The intense competition between these tennis titans has driven the game's evolution, pushing players to innovate and adapt their strategies constantly. As we look to the future, there is no doubt that new rivalries will emerge, captivating fans and propelling the sport of tennis to even greater heights.

The Modern Masters: Tennis Legends of the 21st Century

As the new millennium dawned, the world of tennis witnessed the rise of a new generation of players who would redefine the sport. These modern masters have displayed exceptional skill and talent on the court and captivated fans with their charisma, sportsmanship, and dedication to the game. In this section, we will delve into the careers of some of the most iconic tennis legends of the 21st century.

First and foremost, we must echo the "Big Three" of men's tennis: Roger Federer, Rafael Nadal, and Novak Djokovic. These three players have dominated the sport for nearly two decades, amassing an astonishing number of Grand Slam titles and breaking numerous records. Their unique playing styles, fierce rivalries, and mutual respect for one another have made them fan favorites and have elevated the sport to new heights.

Swiss maestro Roger Federer, often regarded as the greatest tennis player of all time, has mesmerized fans with his elegant playing style, exceptional shot-making, and graceful movement on the court. With 20 Grand Slam titles to his name, Federer's longevity and consistency have earned him a special place in the hearts of tennis enthusiasts worldwide.

Rafael Nadal, the "King of Clay," has reigned supreme on the red dirt of Roland Garros, winning an unprecedented 13 French Open titles. The Spaniard's relentless work ethic, ferocious topspin forehand, and never-say-die attitude have made him a formidable opponent on all surfaces. His 20 Grand Slam titles place him alongside Federer in the annals of tennis history.

Serbian superstar Novak Djokovic has carved his own path to greatness with his incredible athleticism, flexibility, and mental fortitude. With 20 Grand Slam titles, Djokovic has consistently challenged Federer and Nadal for the top spot in the rankings. His remarkable ability to excel under pressure has earned him a reputation as one of the sport's most clutch performers.

On the women's side, Serena Williams has undoubtedly been the most dominant force in tennis over the past two decades. With 23 Grand Slam singles titles, the American powerhouse has shattered records and inspired a new generation of female athletes with her fierce competitiveness, powerful serve, and relentless pursuit of excellence. Serena's impact on the sport extends beyond the court, as she has also been a trailblazer for women's rights and racial equality in sports.

Other notable tennis legends of the 21st century include Venus Williams, Maria Sharapova, Andy Murray, and Stan Wawrinka, all of whom have left indelible marks on the sport with their Grand Slam victories, memorable rivalries, and unique playing styles.

In conclusion, the 21st century has been a golden age for tennis, with the emergence of numerous legends who have captivated fans and elevated the sport to new levels of popularity and excellence. Yet, as we continue to marvel at the exploits of these modern masters, we can only wonder what the future holds for the ever-evolving world of tennis.

The Record Breakers: Tennis Players Who Made History

Tennis, a sport that has captivated the hearts and minds of millions, has seen its fair share of extraordinary athletes who have pushed the boundaries of what was once thought possible. These record-breakers have etched their names in the annals of tennis history, leaving behind a legacy that will be remembered for generations. This section will delve into the remarkable achievements of some of the most iconic tennis players who have shattered records and redefined the game.

One cannot discuss tennis record breakers without mentioning the Swiss maestro, Roger Federer. With 20 Grand Slam titles, Federer holds the record for a male player's most Grand Slam titles. His incredible consistency and longevity in the sport have also earned him the record for the most consecutive weeks spent as the world number one, a staggering 237 weeks. Federer's elegant playing style and unmatched skill have made him a fan favorite and a true game legend.

On the women's side, Serena Williams has been a dominant force in tennis for over two decades. With 23 Grand Slam singles titles, she holds the record for the most Grand Slam titles won in the Open Era. Williams has also achieved a remarkable feat known as the "Serena Slam," winning all four Grand Slam titles in a row, albeit not in the same calendar year. Her powerful serve, aggressive playing style, and sheer determination have made her one of history's most successful and influential tennis players.

Another record-breaker in tennis is the indomitable Rafael Nadal, known as the "King of Clay" for his unparalleled success on clay courts. Nadal holds the record for the most titles won at a single Grand Slam tournament, with an astonishing 13 French Open titles. His relentless work ethic, exceptional athleticism, and fierce competitiveness have made him a formidable opponent and a true tennis icon.

The legendary Martina Navratilova, one of the most successful female tennis players, holds numerous records. Navratilova has 59

Grand Slam titles across singles, doubles, and mixed doubles. Navratilova has the most Grand Slam titles in tennis history. Her incredible versatility and adaptability on the court, combined with her unwavering dedication to the sport, have made her a true trailblazer and an inspiration to countless aspiring tennis players.

These record-breakers have not only made history with their extraordinary achievements but have also inspired millions of fans and players around the world. Their relentless pursuit of excellence, passion for the game, and indomitable spirit have left an indelible mark on tennis. As we continue to marvel at their accomplishments, we are reminded of the power of determination, hard work, and the unyielding belief in one's abilities. These tennis legends have truly redefined the game and will forever be remembered as the ultimate record-breakers in tennis.

The Style Icons: Tennis Legends Who Transformed the Sport's Fashion

Tennis, as a sport, has always been associated with style and elegance. Over the years, numerous tennis legends have not only made their mark on the court but also in the world of fashion. These style icons have transformed how tennis players dress, leaving an indelible mark on the sport's fashion. In this section, we will explore some of the most iconic tennis legends who have revolutionized the sport's fashion and made it an integral part of the game.

Suzanne Lenglen: The Original Tennis Fashionista

The first tennis player to make a statement with her on-court attire was French tennis legend Suzanne Lenglen. In the 1920s, Lenglen broke away from the traditional, restrictive tennis attire of ankle-length skirts and long-sleeved blouses. Instead, she chose daring, knee-length pleated skirts and sleeveless tops designed by French couturier Jean Patou. Lenglen's bold fashion choices made her stand out on the court and allowed her greater freedom of movement, contributing to her success as a player. Her influence on tennis fashion is still felt today, as modern players continue to push the boundaries of style and functionality in their attire.

Billie Jean King: A Trailblazer for Women's Tennis Fashion

Billie Jean King, one of the most influential female tennis players of all time, pioneered in tennis fashion. In the 1960s and 1970s, King challenged the traditional, conservative dress codes for women in tennis by wearing colorful, eye-catching outfits that reflected her vibrant personality. King's fashion choices were stylish and practical, as she often opted for clothing that allowed for greater mobility on the court. Her influence on tennis fashion paved the way for future generations of female players to express themselves through their on-court attire.

Bjorn Borg: The Ice-Cool Style Icon

Swedish tennis legend Bjorn Borg was known for his incredible skill on the court and his distinctive sense of style. Borg's signature look, which included headbands, wristbands, and Fila tracksuits, became synonymous with the cool, collected demeanor that earned him the nickname "Ice Man." Borg's fashion choices were functional and fashionable, as his headbands helped keep sweat out of his eyes during intense matches, while his tracksuits symbolized his laid-back, effortless style. Borg's influence on tennis fashion can still be seen today, with many players adopting similar headbands and wristbands as part of their on-court attire.

Andre Agassi: The Tennis Rebel

In the 1990s, American tennis star Andre Agassi took the tennis world by storm with his rebellious attitude and bold fashion choices. Agassi's iconic look, which included denim shorts, neon-colored shirts, and a wild, untamed mullet, starkly contrasted the more traditional, conservative attire his contemporaries wore. Agassi's fashion choices reflected his larger-than-life personality and helped make him one of the most recognizable and beloved figures in the sport. Although Agassi eventually traded in his denim shorts for more conventional tennis attire, his impact on the sport's fashion is still felt today as players continue to experiment with bold colors and unconventional styles.

Serena Williams: The Modern Tennis Fashion Icon

In recent years, few tennis players have had as significant an impact on the sport's fashion as Serena Williams. The American tennis legend has consistently pushed the boundaries of style on the court, wearing everything from catsuits to tutus in her quest for fashion and functionality. Williams' fashion choices have made her stand out on the court and inspired countless other players to embrace their unique sense of style. As a result, tennis fashion has become more diverse and inclusive, reflecting the wide range of personalities and backgrounds that make up the sport.

In conclusion, the style icons of tennis have played a significant role in shaping the sport's fashion, making it an integral part of the game. From Suzanne Lenglen's daring skirts to Serena Williams' bold catsuits, these tennis legends have transformed how players dress and express themselves on the court. Their influence on tennis fashion has made the sport more visually appealing and allowed players to showcase their individuality and creativity, making tennis a truly unique and captivating spectator sport.

The Inspirational Stories: Overcoming Adversity on the Tennis Court

Like any other sport, tennis is filled with stories of triumph and defeat, of players who have faced seemingly insurmountable challenges and emerged victorious. These inspirational stories serve as a testament to the resilience and determination of the human spirit, and they remind us that anything is possible with hard work and perseverance. This section will explore some of the most remarkable tales of adversity and triumph on the tennis court.

One of the most well-known stories of overcoming adversity in tennis is that of Monica Seles. A prodigious talent, Seles became the youngest-ever French Open champion at the age of 16 in 1990. However, her career took a tragic turn in 1993 when a deranged fan stabbed her during a match in Hamburg. The attack scarred her physically and emotionally, and many doubted whether she would return to the sport. But Seles refused to be defeated. After a two-year hiatus, she returned to tennis triumphantly, winning the 1995 Canadian Open and reaching the final of the US Open that same year. Her incredible comeback is a powerful reminder of the strength of the human spirit.

Another inspiring story is that of Arthur Ashe, the first African American man to win a Grand Slam title. Ashe faced numerous obstacles throughout his career, including racial discrimination and limited access to tennis facilities. Yet, despite these challenges, he persevered and won three Grand Slam titles, including the 1968 US Open, the 1970 Australian Open, and the 1975 Wimbledon. Ashe's success on the court helped break down racial barriers in the sport and paved the way for future generations of African American tennis players.

The tale of Venus and Serena Williams is another example of overcoming adversity in tennis. Raised in the crime-ridden neighborhood of Compton, California, the sisters were introduced to tennis by their father, who saw the sport as a way to escape poverty and violence. Despite their humble beginnings and limited resources, Venus and Serena became two of the most successful and dominant players in the history of women's tennis. Their journey from the streets of Compton to the top of the tennis world is a testament to the power of determination and hard work.

Lastly, we cannot forget the story of Novak Djokovic, who grew up in war-torn Serbia during the 1990s. Amidst the chaos and uncertainty of his childhood, Djokovic found solace in tennis and quickly rose through the ranks to become one of the sport's greatest players. His journey from a war-torn country to the pinnacle of tennis serves as an inspiration to millions around the world.

These stories of overcoming adversity on the tennis court remind us that, no matter the obstacles we face, we have the power to rise above them and achieve greatness. Furthermore, the resilience and determination displayed by these tennis legends serve as a shining example for aspiring players and fans alike, proving that anything is possible with hard work, perseverance, and a never-give-up attitude.

The Future of Tennis: Up-and-Coming Players to Watch

As we celebrate the incredible achievements of tennis legends from the past and present, it is equally important to look toward the future of the sport. The tennis world is brimming with young talent, poised to make their mark on the game and continue the legacy of the greats who came before them. In this section, we will introduce you to some of the most promising up-and-coming players who are set to become the next generation of tennis legends.

One such rising star is Canada's Felix Auger-Aliassime. Born in 2000, this young prodigy made a name for himself on the ATP tour, reaching multiple finals and consistently demonstrating exceptional skill and athleticism on the court. With a powerful serve and an aggressive baseline game, Auger-Aliassime has the potential to become a dominant force in men's tennis for years to come.

On the women's side, American player Coco Gauff has captured the attention of tennis fans worldwide with her incredible performances at such a young age. Born in 2004, Gauff made history in 2019 when she became the youngest player to qualify for the main draw at Wimbledon, where she defeated her idol, Venus Williams, in the first round. With her powerful groundstrokes, impressive court coverage, and unyielding determination, Gauff is undoubtedly a future star to watch.

Another promising talent in men's tennis is Greece's Stefanos Tsitsipas. Born in 1998, Tsitsipas has already achieved significant success on the ATP tour, including multiple titles and a victory over the legendary Roger Federer at the 2019 Australian Open. With his all-court game, exceptional net skills, and charismatic personality, Tsitsipas is poised to become a fan favorite and a formidable contender for Grand Slam titles.

Poland's Iga Swiatek has emerged as a force to be reckoned with in the women's game. Born in 2001, Swiatek burst onto the scene in 2020 when she captured her first Grand Slam title at the French Open, becoming the youngest woman to win the tournament since 1997. With her aggressive baseline play, powerful serve, and remarkable poise under pressure, Swiatek has all the makings of a future tennis legend.

Lastly, we must recognize the potential of Spain's Carlos Alcaraz. Born in 2003, Alcaraz has been hailed as the "next Rafael Nadal" due to his exceptional clay-court prowess and relentless work ethic. With a powerful forehand, impressive court coverage, and a rapidly improving all-court game, Alcaraz is undoubtedly a player to keep an eye on as he continues to climb the ATP rankings.

These young talents represent just a fraction of the promising players who are set to shape the future of tennis. As they continue to develop their skills and make their mark on the sport, we look forward to witnessing the emergence of new rivalries, record-breaking performances, and unforgettable moments on the tennis court. The future of tennis is bright, and these up-and-coming players are sure to carry on the legacy of the legends who have come before them.

The Legacy: How Tennis Legends Have Shaped the Sport

Throughout tennis history, the sport has been graced by the presence of extraordinary athletes who have left an indelible mark on the game. These tennis legends have not only entertained and inspired millions of fans around the world, but they have also shaped the sport in ways that continue to resonate today. In this section, we will explore how these iconic players have influenced the game of tennis, both on and off the court.

First and foremost, the past and present tennis legends have raised the bar for athletic excellence. Their relentless pursuit of perfection, incredible skill, and determination has pushed the boundaries of what is possible on the tennis court. From the powerful serves of Serena

Williams to the unparalleled endurance of Rafael Nadal, these athletes have redefined the sport and inspired countless others to follow in their footsteps.

In addition to their athletic prowess, many tennis legends have been trailblazers regarding social and cultural change. For instance, players like Billie Jean King and Arthur Ashe used their platforms to advocate for gender equality and racial justice. Their courage and conviction helped break down barriers within the sport and contributed to broader societal progress.

Moreover, tennis legends have played a crucial role in popularizing the sport and making it more accessible to people from all walks of life. By captivating audiences with their charisma and style, players like Bjorn Borg, Andre Agassi, and Maria Sharapova have attracted new fans and inspired a new generation of players. Furthermore, the philanthropic efforts of legends like Roger Federer and Venus Williams have helped to promote tennis in underprivileged communities and foster greater inclusivity within the sport.

Another significant aspect of the legacy left by tennis legends is their impact on the sport's fashion and aesthetics. From the iconic white outfits of the early 20th century to today's bold and colorful designs, tennis fashion has evolved dramatically over the years. Players like Fred Perry, Rene Lacoste, and Serena Williams have been style icons and launched their own successful clothing lines, further cementing their influence on the sport's fashion.

Lastly, the rivalries between tennis legends have played a pivotal role in shaping the sport's narrative and generating excitement among fans. Classic rivalries like those between Martina Navratilova and Chris Evert or John McEnroe and Bjorn Borg have provided some of the most memorable moments in tennis history. These epic battles have showcased the incredible skill and passion of the players involved and have also served to elevate the sport as a whole.

In conclusion, the legacy of tennis legends extends far beyond their achievements and accolades. Through their exceptional talent, trailblazing efforts, and enduring influence, these iconic players have shaped the sport of tennis in countless ways. As we continue to marvel at today's tennis stars' feats and eagerly anticipate future legends' emergence, we can appreciate the rich history and lasting impact of the racquet masters who have come before them.

The Enduring Impact of Tennis Legends on the Game

As we conclude our journey through the world of tennis legends, we must reflect on these extraordinary athletes' enduring impact on the game. From the sport's early pioneers to the modern masters, each player has left an indelible mark on tennis, shaping its evolution and inspiring generations of fans and players alike.

The tennis legends we have explored in this chapter have demonstrated exceptional skill and talent on the court and transcended the sport itself. They have become cultural icons, symbols of perseverance, and role models for millions worldwide. Their stories of triumph, adversity, and dedication serve as a testament to the power of the human spirit and the pursuit of excellence.

One of the most significant ways these legends have impacted the game is by pushing the boundaries of what is possible in tennis. They have continually raised the bar, setting new records and redefining the limits of human performance. In doing so, they have inspired countless others to strive for greatness and believe in their potential.

Moreover, the rivalries between these tennis titans have fueled the sport's growth and popularity. The epic clashes between players like Bjorn Borg and John McEnroe, Martina Navratilova, Chris Evert, Roger Federer, and Rafael Nadal have captivated audiences worldwide, drawing in new fans and drawing in new fans elevating the sport to new heights. These rivalries have showcased the incredible skill and athleticism of the players involved and highlighted the drama, passion, and emotion that make tennis such a compelling spectacle.

The impact of tennis legends extends beyond the court, as they have used their fame and influence to bring about positive change in the world. Many have become advocates for social causes, using their platforms to raise awareness and funds for various charities and organizations. Others have broken down barriers, challenging societal norms and prejudices and paving the way for greater diversity and inclusion within the sport.

Furthermore, the style and fashion of tennis have been transformed by these legends, who have brought their unique flair and personality to the game. From the classic elegance of players like Rod Laver and Billie Jean King to the bold and vibrant styles of Andre Agassi and Serena Williams, these icons have redefined what it means to be a tennis player off the court.

As we look to the future of tennis, it is clear that the legacy of these legends will continue to shape the sport for years to come. The next generation of players, inspired by the achievements and stories of their heroes, will undoubtedly push the boundaries even further, setting new records and creating unforgettable moments in the annals of tennis history.

In conclusion, the enduring impact of tennis legends on the game is undeniable. They have shaped the sport through their incredible skill and talent and left a lasting legacy that extends far beyond the court. As fans and players alike, we are fortunate to have witnessed the remarkable careers of these extraordinary athletes, and their influence will continue to inspire and captivate future generations of tennis enthusiasts.

9

THE SWEET SCIENCE: BOXING LEGENDS

Boxing, the Sweet Science

Boxing, often referred to as the "Sweet Science," is a sport that has captivated the hearts and minds of millions of fans worldwide for centuries. It is a unique blend of raw power, speed, skill, and strategy, where two combatants face off in a test of physical and mental fortitude. The history of boxing is rich and storied, with its roots dating back to ancient civilizations and evolving into the modern spectacle we know today. This chapter will explore the art and history of boxing, delving into the lives and careers of the sport's most legendary figures.

The origins of boxing can be traced back to ancient Egypt, Greece, and Rome, where it was practiced as entertainment and a means to settle disputes. The sport has since evolved through the ages, with the introduction of gloves, weight classes, and standardized rules. The Marquess of Queensberry Rules, established in 1867, laid the foundation for modern boxing, emphasizing sportsmanship and fair play.

The Golden Age of Boxing, from the early 20th century to the 1960s, saw some of the sport's most iconic figures rise. Pioneers and innovators like Jack Johnson, Joe Louis, and Sugar Ray Robinson broke barriers and set new standards for skill and athleticism in the ring. This era also witnessed the birth of boxing's most storied rivalries, as fighters like Muhammad Ali, Joe Frazier, and George Foreman engaged in epic battles that captivated audiences worldwide.

Throughout its history, boxing has been divided into various weight classes, each with its unique blend of power, speed, and skill. From the heavyweight titans who ruled the ring with their devastating power to the lightning-fast lightweight fighters who dazzled fans with speed and agility, each division has produced its own legendary champions.

The sport of boxing has not been without its share of controversy and adversity. For example, the rise of women's boxing has been met with both support and resistance, as female fighters like Christy Martin and Laila Ali fought to break down barriers and prove their worth in a male-dominated sport. Additionally, the role of trainers and mentors in shaping the careers of boxing's greatest legends cannot be understated, as these behind-the-scenes figures have played a crucial role in developing their fighters' skills and strategies.

Boxing's impact on society extends far beyond the confines of the ring. The sport has been a powerful symbol of perseverance, determination, and triumph in the face of adversity, inspiring countless individuals to overcome their own challenges. Furthermore, the stories of boxing's greatest legends have transcended the sport, becoming ingrained in popular culture through films, books, and other forms of media.

As we look to the future of boxing, the sport continues to evolve and produce new stars who carry on the legacy of the legends who came before them. With advancements in training methods, technology, and a growing global audience, the Sweet Science remains a captivating and enduring spectacle that will continue to shape and inspire future generations.

In this chapter, we will delve deeper into the lives and careers of the most legendary figures in the history of boxing. From the pioneers who laid the groundwork for the sport to the modern-day warriors who continue to push the boundaries of what is possible in the ring, these are the stories of the men and women who have left an indelible mark on Sweet Science.

The Golden Age of Boxing: Pioneers and Innovators

The Golden Age of Boxing, spanning from the early 1900s to the 1960s, was when the sport truly captured the hearts and minds of the public. This era saw the rise of some of the most iconic and influential figures in boxing history, whose impact on the sport can still be felt today. These pioneers and innovators showcased their incredible skills in the ring and played a significant role in shaping the sport's rules, techniques, and global appeal.

One of the most prominent figures of this era was Jack Johnson, the first African-American heavyweight champion of the world. Johnson's reign from 1908 to 1915 was marked by his exceptional skill, power, and defensive prowess. His victories against white opponents, particularly his defeat of James J. Jeffries in the "Fight of the Century" in 1910, broke racial barriers and paved the way for future black champions.

Another trailblazer of the Golden Age was Jack Dempsey, the "Manassa Mauler," who held the heavyweight title from 1919 to 1926. Dempsey's aggressive, relentless style and devastating punching power made him a fan favorite and a box-office draw. His legendary bouts against Georges Carpentier and Gene Tunney were among the first to generate million-dollar gates, ushering in a new era of commercial success for the sport.

Benny Leonard and Henry Armstrong stood out as true innovators in the lighter-weight classes. Leonard, a lightweight champion from 1917 to 1925, was known for his incredible ring intelligence and tactical prowess. He is often credited with developing the modern boxing style, emphasizing speed, footwork, and combination punching. On the other hand, Armstrong achieved the remarkable feat of holding world titles in three different weight classes simultaneously (featherweight, lightweight, and welterweight) in the late 1930s. His relentless pressure and non-stop punching style inspired generations of fighters to come.

The Golden Age also saw the rise of the legendary Joe Louis, the "Brown Bomber," who held the heavyweight title for an unprecedented 11 years and 25 successful defenses from 1937 to 1949. Louis's powerful punches and impeccable technique made him one of the most dominant champions in history. His victories, particularly his knockout of German Max Schmeling in 1938, transcended the sport and became symbols of American pride and resistance against the rise of fascism in Europe.

The pioneers and innovators of the Golden Age of Boxing laid the foundation for the sport's growth and development in the following decades. Their remarkable achievements, both inside and outside the ring, inspire and influence today's boxers. As we delve deeper into the legends of boxing, it is essential to remember and appreciate the contributions of these trailblazers who helped shape the Sweet Science into the global phenomenon it is today.

Heavyweight Heroes: The Titans of the Ring

The heavyweight division has always been the most captivating and awe-inspiring category in boxing. With their immense power and larger-than-life personas, these titans of the ring have captured the imagination of fans and the general public alike. This section will delve into the lives and careers of some of the most iconic heavyweight heroes who have left an indelible mark on the sport.

One cannot discuss heavyweight boxing without mentioning the legendary Muhammad Ali. Born Cassius Marcellus Clay Jr., Ali was a phenomenal athlete and a cultural icon who transcended the sport. Ali became a three-time world heavyweight champion and an Olympic gold medalist with his lightning-fast footwork, powerful punches, and unparalleled charisma. His fights against formidable opponents such as Joe Frazier, George Foreman, and Sonny Liston are etched in boxing history. Ali's unwavering confidence and famous catchphrase, "float like a butterfly, sting like a bee," continue inspiring generations of boxers and fans.

Another heavyweight hero who dominated the boxing world was Joe Louis, the "Brown Bomber." Louis held the world heavyweight title for an astounding 140 consecutive months, defending it 25 times. His powerful punches and stoic demeanor made him a force to be reckoned with in the ring. Louis's most famous fight was against German boxer Max Schmeling in 1938, which was seen as a symbolic battle between democracy and fascism during the tense pre-World War II era. Louis's victory made him a national hero and a symbol of hope for many Americans.

The 1990s saw the rise of the fearsome and controversial Mike Tyson. Known as "Iron Mike," Tyson became the youngest heavyweight champion in history at 20. His ferocious fighting style, marked by relentless aggression and devastating knockout power, made him one of the most feared and respected boxers of his time. Unfortunately, Tyson's tumultuous personal life and legal troubles often overshadowed his achievements in the ring, but his impact on the sport remains undeniable.

In recent years, the heavyweight division has been revitalized by Wladimir and Vitali Klitschko, two Ukrainian brothers who dominated the division for over a decade. Their size, power, and technical skill made them formidable opponents and helped to rekindle interest in heavyweight boxing. The current crop of heavyweight heroes, including Anthony Joshua, Tyson Fury, and Deontay Wilder, are carrying on the legacy of these greats, ensuring that the heavyweight division remains the most thrilling and captivating weight class in boxing.

The heavyweight heroes mentioned here and countless others have contributed to the rich tapestry of boxing history. Their incredible feats of strength, skill, and determination have left an indelible mark on the sport and have inspired countless individuals to step into the ring and chase their dreams. As we continue to witness the rise of new heavyweight stars, we can only hope that they will carry on the legacy of these titans of the ring and further elevate the sweet science of boxing.

Middleweight Masters: The Perfect Balance of Power and Speed

The middleweight division has long been considered the perfect balance of power and speed in boxing. Middleweight fighters have consistently demonstrated an exceptional blend of technical skill, agility, and raw power by occupying a unique space between the heavyweight bruisers and the lightning-fast lightweights. This chapter will delve into the lives and careers of some of the most iconic middleweight masters, exploring their unique styles, unforgettable bouts, and their indelible impact on boxing.

One cannot discuss the middleweight division without mentioning the legendary Sugar Ray Robinson. Widely regarded as the greatest pound-for-pound boxer of all time, Robinson's incredible speed, precision, and power earned him an astounding 173 victories throughout his career, with 108 coming by knockout. His remarkable six-fight rivalry with fellow middleweight great Jake LaMotta, which included the infamous "St. Valentine's Day Massacre" bout, remains one of the most storied rivalries in boxing history.

Another middleweight master who left an indelible mark on the sport is the Argentinean powerhouse Carlos Monzon. With a professional record of 87 wins, 3 losses, and 9 draws, Monzon held the undisputed middleweight championship for seven years, defending his title 14 times. His relentless, aggressive style and granite chin made him a formidable opponent. His knockout victories over greats like Nino Benvenuti and Emile Griffith solidified his place among the all-time greats.

Marvin Hagler, known as "Marvelous Marvin," is another middleweight legend whose ferocious fighting style and iron will captivate boxing fans worldwide. Hagler's reign as the undisputed middleweight champion lasted for nearly seven years, during which he defended his title 12 times. His epic battle with Thomas "Hitman" Hearns, dubbed "The War," remains one of the most thrilling and brutal bouts in boxing history.

In recent times, the middleweight division has been graced by Bernard Hopkins, whose incredible longevity and defensive prowess made him the oldest world champion in boxing history at 49. Another modern-day middleweight master is Gennady "GGG" Golovkin, whose devastating punching power and relentless pressure have made him one of the most feared fighters of his generation.

The middleweight division has also been home to some of the sport's most memorable and heated rivalries. The aforementioned Sugar Ray Robinson and Jake LaMotta rivalry set the stage for future middleweight clashes, such as the intense battles between Marvin Hagler and Sugar Ray Leonard and the more recent showdowns between Gennady Golovkin and Canelo Alvarez.

Throughout the history of boxing, the middleweight division has produced some of the most iconic and unforgettable fighters and moments. These middleweight masters, with their perfect balance of power and speed, have entertained and inspired generations of fans and left an indelible mark on the sport of boxing. As the sweet science continues to evolve, there is no doubt that the middleweight division will continue to be a breeding ground for legendary fighters and unforgettable battles.

Welterweight Warriors: The Fierce Competitors of a Storied Division

The welterweight division has long been a breeding ground for some of the most skilled and tenacious fighters in the history of boxing. With a weight limit of 147 pounds, welterweights possess a unique blend of speed, power, and agility, producing some of the most memorable bouts and legendary champions the sport has ever seen. This section will delve into the storied history of the welterweight division and pay tribute to the warriors who have left an indelible mark on the sweet science.

The origins of the welterweight division can be traced back to the early 20th century when fighters like Barbados Joe Walcott and Dixie Kid first captured the imagination of boxing fans with their thrilling battles and extraordinary skill. However, it was only with the emergence of the legendary Sugar Ray Robinson in the 1940s that the welterweight division truly came into its own. Robinson, widely regarded as one of the greatest boxers of all time, reigned supreme as the welterweight champion for five years, defeating a who's who of fellow Hall of Famers along the way.

In the following decades, the welterweight division produced iconic champions and unforgettable rivalries. The 1960s and 70s saw the rise of fighters like Emile Griffith, Jose Napoles, and the incomparable Roberto Duran, who would become one of the most feared and respected boxers in history. Duran's epic battles with Sugar Ray Leonard in the 1980s helped to define the era and cement the welterweight division's reputation as a hotbed of talent and excitement.

The 1990s and 2000s ushered in a new generation of welterweight warriors led by Oscar De La Hoya, Felix Trinidad, and Shane Mosley. These fighters, known for their speed, power, and charisma, helped to bring the sport of boxing to new heights of popularity and commercial success. However, the emergence of Floyd Mayweather Jr. and Manny Pacquiao truly set the welterweight division alight. Their long-awaited showdown in 2015, dubbed the "Fight of the Century," captivated the world and showcased the best that the sweet science offers.

The welterweight division has also been a trailblazer when it comes to gender equality in the sport of boxing. Pioneers like Christy Martin and Lucia Rijker paved the way for a new generation of female fighters, including Cecilia Braekhus and Jessica McCaskill, who continue to break down barriers and prove that the welterweight division is not just a man's world.

As we look to the future, the welterweight division remains as competitive and compelling as ever. With rising stars like Errol Spence Jr., Terence Crawford, and Shawn Porter vying for supremacy, there is no shortage of talent and potential for even more legendary battles in the years to come.

In conclusion, the welterweight division has long been a showcase for the very best that the sport of boxing has to offer. From the early pioneers to the modern-day warriors, these fierce competitors have provided fans countless unforgettable moments and etched their names into the annals of boxing history. As we celebrate the legends of the past and look forward to the stars of the future, one thing is sure: the welterweight division will continue to be a source of excitement, inspiration, and awe for generations to come.

Lightweight Legends: The Fast and the Furious

The lightweight division has long been a showcase for some of the most electrifying and awe-inspiring talents in boxing. These fighters, typically weighing 130 and 135 pounds, possess a unique blend of speed, agility, and power that has captivated audiences for generations. In this section, we will delve into the careers of some of the most iconic lightweight legends, exploring their rise to prominence, their signature fighting styles, and their indelible mark on the sport.

One cannot discuss the lightweight division without mentioning the great Benny Leonard, widely regarded as one of the finest boxers of all time. Born in 1896, Leonard's career spanned over two decades, during which he amassed an incredible record of 89 wins, 6 losses, and 1 draw. Known for his exceptional ring intelligence and tactical prowess, Leonard was a master of boxing, able to outthink and outmaneuver his opponents easily. His influence on the sport is still felt today, with many modern fighters citing him as a key inspiration.

Another standout in the lightweight division is the legendary Roberto Duran, a Panamanian fighter whose ferocity and tenacity earned him the nickname "Hands of Stone." Duran's career began in the late 1960s, and he quickly established himself as a force to be reckoned with, capturing the WBA Lightweight title in 1972. Throughout his illustrious career, Duran would win world titles in four different weight classes, a testament to his incredible skill and adaptability.

The 1980s saw the rise of another lightweight icon in the form of Pernell "Sweet Pea" Whitaker, an American fighter known for his slick defensive skills and elusive movement. Whitaker's style was a masterclass in the art of "hit and not get hit," as he would effortlessly slip and slide away from his opponent's attacks while landing pinpoint counterpunches. A four-weight world champion, Whitaker's influence can be seen in the fighting styles of many contemporary boxers, who seek to emulate his defensive wizardry.

In recent years, the lightweight division has continued producing exceptional talents, such as the Ukrainian phenom Vasyl Lomachenko. A two-time Olympic gold medalist, Lomachenko's amateur record is a staggering 396 wins and only 1 loss. Since turning professional, he has continued to dazzle audiences with his sublime footwork, lightning-fast combinations, and unparalleled ring IQ. Already a three-weight world champion, Lomachenko's career is still in its prime, and he is poised to further solidify his status as one of the all-time greats.

The lightweight division has long been a breeding ground for some of the most exciting and dynamic fighters in the history of boxing. From the tactical genius of Benny Leonard to the ferocious power of Roberto Duran, the defensive mastery of Pernell Whitaker to the dazzling skills of Vasyl Lomachenko, these legends have left an indelible mark on the sport. Their incredible achievements testify to the enduring appeal of the sweet science and the limitless potential of those who dare to step into the ring.

The Women of Boxing: Breaking Barriers and Making History

Boxing, often considered a male-dominated sport, has witnessed the rise of numerous female fighters who have defied stereotypes and shattered glass ceilings. These women have showcased their exceptional skills in the ring and played a pivotal role in breaking barriers and making history. This section pays tribute to the trailblazing women of boxing who have left an indelible mark on the sport and inspired countless others to follow in their footsteps.

The journey of women in boxing has been fraught with challenges and obstacles. For decades, female boxers were denied opportunities to compete professionally, and their accomplishments were often overshadowed by their male counterparts. However, the resilience and determination of these women have led to significant milestones in the sport's history.

One of the earliest pioneers of women's boxing was Barbara Buttrick, a British fighter who began her career in the 1940s. Despite standing at just 4'11", Buttrick's tenacity and skill earned her the nickname "The Mighty Atom." She became the first woman to win a world title in 1957, paving the way for future generations of female boxers.

In the 1980s and 1990s, the landscape of women's boxing began to change, with fighters like Christy Martin and Lucia Rijker gaining prominence. Martin, known as "The Coal Miner's Daughter," was a ferocious competitor who captured multiple world titles and became the first woman to sign with legendary promoter Don King. Rijker, a Dutch kickboxing champion, transitioned to boxing and quickly became one of the sport's most feared fighters, earning the moniker "The Most Dangerous Woman in the World."

The turn of the century saw the emergence of Laila Ali, the daughter of boxing icon Muhammad Ali. Laila's entrance into the sport brought unprecedented attention to women's boxing, and she more than lived up to the hype. With a perfect record of 24 wins and no losses, Laila Ali became a multiple-time world champion and a symbol of empowerment for women everywhere.

The sport has continued to evolve in recent years, with female boxers like Claressa Shields, Katie Taylor, and Amanda Serrano making headlines and breaking records. Shields, a two-time Olympic gold medalist, has already captured world titles in multiple weight classes and is regarded as one of the best female fighters ever. Taylor, an Irish sensation, has unified world titles in the lightweight division and is a trailblazer for women's boxing in her home country. Serrano, a Puerto Rican powerhouse, has won world titles in an astonishing seven weight classes, showcasing her incredible versatility and skill.

The women of boxing have excelled in the ring and played a crucial role in breaking barriers and making history. Their achievements have paved the way for future generations of female fighters, and their impact on the sport is undeniable. As the sweet science continues to evolve, there is no doubt that women's boxing will continue to grow and inspire countless others to challenge conventions and reach for greatness.

The Greatest Rivalries: Epic Battles That Defined the Sport

Boxing is a sport that thrives on the intensity of competition, and nothing captures the imagination of fans more than a great rivalry. Throughout the history of the sweet science, numerous epic battles have not only defined the careers of the fighters involved but have also left an indelible mark on the sport itself. This section will explore some of the most iconic rivalries that have shaped the boxing world and provided fans with unforgettable moments of drama, skill, and courage.

One of the most storied rivalries in boxing history is the trilogy of fights between Muhammad Ali and Joe Frazier. Known as the "Fight of the Century," their first encounter in 1971 saw two undefeated heavyweight champions going head-to-head in a battle for the ages. Frazier emerged victorious in this first bout, handing Ali his first professional loss. However, Ali would go on to win their next two fights, including the legendary "Thrilla in Manila" in 1975, widely regarded as one of the greatest fights of all time. The intensity and animosity between these two titans of the ring made their rivalry a defining moment in the sport's history.

Another classic rivalry that captivated the boxing world was the series of fights between Sugar Ray Leonard, Thomas Hearns, Marvin Hagler, and Roberto Duran, collectively known as "The Four Kings." These four fighters dominated the welterweight and middleweight divisions during the 1980s, and their battles against each other produced some of the most memorable moments in boxing history. The fights between Leonard and Hearns, in particular, showcased the perfect blend of power, speed, and technical skill that made them both legends of the sport.

In more recent times, the rivalry between Mexican warriors Marco Antonio Barrera and Erik Morales produced a trilogy of fights that will forever be remembered for their ferocity and heart. These two fighters, who genuinely disliked each other, engaged in three brutal wars that showcased their incredible skill, determination, and courage. Their first fight in 2000, which Morales won by a controversial split decision, is considered one of the best fights of the 21st century.

The world of women's boxing has also seen its share of great rivalries, perhaps the most famous being the battles between Christy Martin and Laila Ali. The two fighters, both trailblazers for women in the sport, faced off in a highly anticipated bout in 2003. Ali, the daughter of the legendary Muhammad Ali, emerged victorious, cementing her status as one of the greatest female fighters ever.

These rivalries and countless others have played a crucial role in shaping the sport of boxing and creating the legends that we celebrate today. The passion, skill, and determination displayed by these fighters in their epic battles have not only inspired future generations of boxers but have also left an indelible mark on the hearts and minds of fans worldwide. As the sport continues to evolve, there is no doubt that new rivalries will emerge, providing us with even more unforgettable moments and further solidifying the enduring legacy of boxing's greatest legends.

The Trainers and Mentors: The Architects Behind the Legends

Behind every great boxer stands a trainer or mentor who has played an instrumental role in shaping their career. These architects of legends have honed the physical skills of their protégés and instilled in them the mental fortitude and strategic acumen necessary to excel in the ring. This section pays tribute to the unsung heroes of the sweet science, the trainers, and mentors who have molded raw talent into legendary champions.

The role of a boxing trainer extends far beyond teaching the basic techniques of the sport. They are responsible for developing a fighter's unique style, identifying their strengths and weaknesses, and devising strategies to exploit their opponent's vulnerabilities. Moreover, trainers often serve as father figures, confidants, and life coaches, guiding their fighters through the highs and lows of their careers.

One of the most iconic trainers in boxing history is Angelo Dundee, who guided the careers of two of the sport's greatest legends, Muhammad Ali and Sugar Ray Leonard. Dundee's keen eye for detail and ability to adapt his fighters' styles to opponents made him an invaluable asset in their corners. In addition, his calm demeanor and unwavering belief in his fighters' abilities instilled confidence in them, allowing them to perform at their best in the most crucial moments.

Another legendary trainer is Emanuel Steward, known for his work with heavyweight champions Lennox Lewis and Wladimir Klitschko. Steward's expertise in developing a fighter's power and technical skills, combined with his astute tactical mind, made him one of the most sought-after trainers in the sport. His ability to transform fighters into disciplined, focused, and relentless competitors earned him a place among the pantheon of boxing's greatest mentors.

Cus D'Amato, the man behind the rise of the youngest heavyweight champion in history, Mike Tyson, was a master of the psychological aspects of boxing. D'Amato's unique training methods, which included hypnosis and visualization techniques, helped to instill an unshakable self-belief in his fighters. His emphasis on mental preparation and developing a strong will to win set his protégés apart from their peers.

The world of women's boxing has also seen its share of influential trainers and mentors. Ann Wolfe, a former world champion herself, has become one of the most respected trainers in the sport, working with fighters such as James Kirkland and Marlen Esparza. Wolfe's no-nonsense approach and dedication to her fighters' success have made her a trailblazer in a male-dominated field.

The impact of these trainers and mentors on their fighters' careers cannot be overstated. They have not only shaped the physical and mental abilities of their protégés but also left an indelible mark on the sport of boxing. Their dedication, passion, and expertise have been crucial in developing the legends we revere today. Their influence will continue to be felt in future generations of fighters.

The Cultural Impact of Boxing: How the Sweet Science Shaped Society

Boxing, often referred to as the "Sweet Science," has profoundly impacted society throughout its storied history. From its ancient origins to the modern era, the sport has transcended the boundaries of the ring and left an indelible mark on culture, politics, and the human spirit. In this section, we will explore how boxing has shaped society and contributed to our collective understanding of courage, resilience, and the pursuit of greatness.

The cultural impact of boxing can be traced back to its earliest days when it was practiced as entertainment and a test of strength and skill among ancient civilizations. The Greeks, for instance, included boxing in the Olympic Games as early as 688 BC, and the Romans later adopted the sport as a popular spectacle in their gladiatorial contests. These early iterations of boxing served as a means of entertainment and a reflection of societal values and norms, such as physical prowess, courage, and honor.

As the sport evolved over the centuries, it continued to captivate audiences and inspire generations of fighters and fans. The advent of professional boxing in the 18th and 19th centuries brought with it a new level of public interest and excitement, as well as a growing awareness of the social and political implications of the sport. Boxing matches often served as a microcosm of larger societal issues, with fighters representing different ethnic, national, and social groups vying for supremacy in the ring.

In the 20th century, boxing emerged as a powerful symbol of resistance and empowerment for marginalized communities. Fighters like Jack Johnson, the first African American heavyweight champion, and Joe Louis, whose victory over German Max Schmeling in 1938 was a triumph over Nazi ideology, used their success in the ring to challenge racial and political barriers. Similarly, the legendary Muhammad Ali became a global icon for his extraordinary skills as a boxer and for his outspoken activism on issues such as civil rights, religious freedom, and opposition to the Vietnam War.

Boxing has also significantly shaped popular culture, with countless films, books, and songs inspired by the sport and its larger-than-life personalities. From classic movies like "Rocky" and "Raging Bull" to literary works such as Ernest Hemingway's "The Old Man and the Sea" and Joyce Carol Oates' "On Boxing," the sport has served as a powerful metaphor for the human struggle and the triumph of the underdog. Moreover, the iconic image of the boxer – bloodied, battered, but unbowed – has become a symbol of resilience and determination in the face of adversity.

In recent years, the sport has continued to evolve and adapt to the changing landscape of society, with the rise of women's boxing and the increasing prominence of fighters from diverse backgrounds and nationalities. As the Sweet Science moves forward, it remains a testament to the enduring appeal of competition, the pursuit of excellence, and the indomitable human spirit.

In conclusion, the cultural impact of boxing extends far beyond the confines of the ring. The sport has served as a mirror for society, reflecting our values, aspirations, and struggles while providing a platform for individuals to challenge conventions and break down barriers. As we celebrate the legends of the Sweet Science, we also pay tribute to the transformative power of boxing and its enduring legacy in shaping the world around us.

The Future of Boxing: Rising Stars and the Evolution of the Sport

As we look back at the rich history of boxing and the legends who have graced the ring, it is essential to look forward and consider the future of this storied sport. The Sweet Science continues to evolve, with new talents emerging and the sport itself adapting to the changing landscape of the athletic world. In this section, we will explore the rising stars poised to become the next generation of boxing legends and how the sport is evolving to meet the demands of the modern era.

The boxing world is always full of talent, and the current crop of rising stars is no exception. These young fighters come from diverse backgrounds and possess a wide range of skills, but they all share a common goal: to etch their names alongside the sport's legends. Some of the most promising talents include Shakur Stevenson, a lightning-fast featherweight with a penchant for precision; Teofimo Lopez, a hard-hitting lightweight with a flair for the dramatic; and Vergil Ortiz Jr., a welterweight powerhouse with a relentless work ethic. These fighters and many others are poised to carry the torch for the sport and inspire a new generation of fans.

As these rising stars continue to develop and make their mark on the sport, boxing is also evolving. The increased focus on fighter safety is one of the most significant changes in recent years. With a greater understanding of the long-term effects of head trauma, the boxing community has taken steps to minimize the risk of injury, such as implementing stricter medical protocols and emphasizing proper techniques in training. This shift in focus protects the athletes and ensures that the sport remains viable and respected in the broader athletic community.

Another notable development in the world of boxing is the increasing popularity of women's boxing. Pioneers like Christy Martin, Laila Ali, and Ann Wolfe paved the way for a new generation of female fighters now enjoying greater visibility and opportunities than ever before. In addition, fighters like Claressa Shields, Katie Taylor, and Amanda Serrano are breaking barriers and proving that women's boxing can be just as exciting and competitive as the men's side of the sport.

Finally, the future of boxing is shaped by the rise of new media and technology. The internet and social media have allowed greater access to fights and behind-the-scenes content, fostering a more engaged and informed fanbase. Additionally, advancements in training technology and sports science are helping fighters to optimize their performance and extend their careers. As the sport adapts to these changes, seeing how Sweet Science evolves in the coming years will be fascinating.

In conclusion, the future of boxing is bright, with a new generation of talented fighters ready to make their mark on the sport and carry on the legacy of the legends who came before them. As the sport continues to evolve and adapt to the modern era, it is clear that the Sweet Science will remain a vital and captivating part of the athletic world for years.

The Enduring Legacy of Boxing's Greatest Legends

As we reach the end of our journey through the annals of boxing history, reflecting on the enduring legacy of the sport's greatest legends is essential. These exceptional athletes have left an indelible mark on the world of boxing and have transcended the boundaries of the sport to become cultural icons and symbols of inspiration for generations to come.

The stories of these boxing legends are a testament to the power of determination, resilience, and the indomitable human spirit. They have faced adversity inside and outside the ring and emerged as champions, leaving behind a trail of unforgettable moments and awe-inspiring performances. Their impact on the sport is immeasurable, as they have inspired countless young fighters to lace up their gloves and pursue their dreams of boxing glory.

The legacy of these legends is not limited to their achievements in the ring. They have also played a significant role in shaping society's perception of the sport and its athletes. Through their charisma, intelligence, and eloquence, they have demonstrated that boxers are not just one-dimensional warriors but complex individuals with unique stories to tell. They have used their fame and influence to advocate for social change, promote philanthropy, and challenge stereotypes, thus leaving a lasting impact on the world beyond the confines of the boxing ring.

Moreover, the rivalries and epic battles that have defined the sport have become integral to boxing's rich history. These unforgettable clashes have showcased the highest levels of skill, courage, and determination but have also served as a reminder of the importance of sportsmanship, respect, and camaraderie among competitors. The rivalries have captivated audiences worldwide, creating a shared experience transcending borders, languages, and cultures.

The trainers and mentors who have guided these legends throughout their careers also deserve recognition for their invaluable contributions to the sport. Their wisdom, experience, and unwavering support have been instrumental in shaping the careers of these exceptional athletes. They have honed their fighters' skills and instilled in them the values of discipline, humility, and perseverance, which are essential for success both inside and outside the ring.

As we look to the future of boxing, it is evident that the sport will continue to evolve and produce new stars who will carry the torch of greatness. The lessons learned from the legends of the past will undoubtedly serve as a blueprint for the champions of tomorrow. The sweet science will persist in captivating the hearts and minds of fans across the globe, as it has done for centuries.

In conclusion, the enduring legacy of boxing's greatest legends is a testament to the power of the human spirit and the universal appeal of the sweet science. Their stories of triumph, adversity, and perseverance will continue to inspire and captivate future generations. As we celebrate their achievements and remember their contributions to the sport, we are reminded of the timeless allure of boxing and its unique ability to unite people from all walks of life in their shared passion for the sweet science.

10

THE ULTIMATE COMPETITORS: LEGENDS FROM VARIOUS SPORTS

Celebration in Victory

The world of sports has always been a stage for extraordinary athleticism, skill, and determination feats. Throughout history, athletes have pushed the boundaries of human potential, captivating audiences with their incredible performances and inspiring countless others to strive for greatness. This book will explore the lives and achievements of 100+ sports legends who have left an indelible mark on their respective disciplines. These athletes embody the spirit of competition, demonstrating the power of perseverance, hard work, and an unwavering commitment to excellence.

The ultimate competitors we will celebrate in this book come from a diverse range of sports, from the elegance and precision of tennis to the raw power and aggression of boxing. Each of these legends has faced unique challenges and obstacles, but they all share a common thread: an unyielding drive to be the best. Their stories are not just about winning championships and breaking records; they are about the transformative power of sports and the impact these athletes have had on the world beyond the playing field.

In the following chapters, we will delve into the lives and careers of these remarkable individuals, exploring the qualities that set them apart from their peers and the moments that defined their legacies. We will examine the rivalries that fueled their competitive fires, the setbacks that tested their resolve, and the triumphs cemented their historical places.

From the titans of tennis to the pioneers of extreme sports, these legends represent the pinnacle of human achievement in their respective fields. They have inspired generations of fans and fellow athletes with their passion, skill, and indomitable spirit. As we journey through the world of sports and the stories of these extraordinary competitors, we will discover the qualities that make them true legends and the enduring lessons they can teach us about the power of competition and the human spirit.

So, let us embark on this exciting journey, celebrating the spirit of competition and the incredible athletes who have made their mark on the world of sports. Through their stories, we will gain a deeper appreciation for the dedication, sacrifice, and heart it takes to become a legend and the lasting impact these remarkable individuals have had on the world around them.

The Titans of Tennis: Unmatched Skill and Passion

The world of tennis has been graced by numerous legends who have left an indelible mark on the sport. These titans of tennis have showcased their unmatched skill and passion on the court and have inspired generations of players and fans alike. In this section, we will delve into the lives and careers of some of the most iconic tennis legends, exploring their incredible achievements and the qualities that set them apart.

First and foremost, we must pay homage to the legendary Rod Laver, the Australian maestro who remains the only player in history to have won the Grand Slam – all four major tennis championships in a single calendar year – twice, in 1962 and 1969. Laver's aggressive serve-and-volley style, extraordinary athleticism, and relentless determination made him a formidable force on the court.

Another tennis titan is the incomparable Martina Navratilova, who dominated the women's game in the 1970s and 1980s. With a record 59 Grand Slam titles across singles, doubles, and mixed doubles, Navratilova's versatility and competitive spirit remain unparalleled. Her fierce rivalry with Chris Evert, another tennis legend, captivated fans and elevated the sport to new heights.

The 1990s saw the emergence of two more tennis greats: Pete Sampras and Steffi Graf. Sampras, known for his powerful serve and exceptional net play, held the record for the most Grand Slam singles titles (14) until Roger Federer surpassed it. On the other hand, Graf remains the only player to have won each of the four major championships at least four times. Her fluid movement, powerful forehand, and unwavering focus made her a force to be reckoned with on the court.

Recently, the tennis world has been enthralled by the "Big Three" – Roger Federer, Rafael Nadal, and Novak Djokovic. These three players have amassed an astonishing number of Grand Slam titles and consistently pushed the sport's boundaries with their incredible skill, passion, and sportsmanship. Federer's elegant playing style, Nadal's ferocious intensity, and Djokovic's unparalleled consistency have made them true icons of the game.

Serena Williams has reigned supreme on the women's side, amassing an astounding 23 Grand Slam singles titles and counting. Her powerful serve, aggressive baseline play, and sheer determination have made her one of the most dominant athletes in the sport's history.

These titans of tennis have left an indelible mark on the sport, inspiring countless players and fans with their skill, passion, and dedication. Their achievements testify to the power of hard work, perseverance, and the unyielding spirit of competition. As we continue to marvel at their accomplishments and celebrate their legacies, we are reminded of the true essence of tennis. This sport transcends boundaries and unites people from all walks of life in their shared love for the game.

Basketball's Greatest: Soaring to New Heights

Basketball, a sport that has captivated the hearts and minds of fans across the globe, has produced some of the most awe-inspiring athletes in history. These legends have displayed exceptional skill and talent on the court and embody the spirit of competition, pushing the boundaries of what is possible in the game. This section will pay tribute to the greatest basketball players who have soared to new heights and left an indelible mark on the sport.

The conversation about basketball's greatest must begin with the iconic Michael Jordan. Known as "His Airness," Jordan's gravity-defying dunks, unmatched scoring ability, and relentless pursuit of victory symbolized excellence in the sport. Jordan's impact on the game is undeniable, with six NBA championships, five MVP awards, and ten scoring titles. His competitive drive and unwavering determination to win inspired a generation of players and fans alike.

Another legend who has left an indelible mark on the sport is

Magic Johnson. Johnson revolutionized the game as a point guard with his incredible court vision, dazzling passes, and unmatched leadership. His rivalry with Larry Bird, another all-time great, fueled the growth of the NBA in the 1980s. Together, they elevated the sport to new heights, captivating fans with intense battles on the court. Bird's sharpshooting, basketball IQ, and clutch performances made him a force to be reckoned with, earning him three NBA championships and three MVP awards.

In more recent times, the basketball world has been graced by the talents of LeBron James, a player who has consistently defied expectations and shattered records. James has dominated the game for nearly two decades with his unique combination of size, speed, and skill. His ability to play multiple positions, score at will, and make his teammates better have earned him four NBA championships and four MVP awards. As he continues to etch his name in the annals of basketball history, James' legacy as one of the greatest to ever play the game is solidified.

The list of basketball legends would be incomplete without mentioning the late, great Kobe Bryant. Known as the "Black Mamba," Bryant's relentless work ethic, killer instinct, and unparalleled footwork made him one of the most feared competitors in the sport. With five NBA championships and an MVP award, Bryant's impact on the game will forever be remembered.

These legends and countless others have shaped the game of basketball into what it is today. Their passion, skill, and dedication to the sport have inspired millions worldwide, leaving a lasting legacy that will continue to influence future generations of players. As we celebrate these ultimate competitors, we are reminded of the power of sports to unite, inspire, and bring out the best in all of us.

Soccer Superstars: Masters of the Beautiful Game

Soccer, or football as it is known in most parts of the world, is a sport that has captured the hearts and minds of millions. The game transcends borders, languages, and cultures, uniting people through their shared love for the beautiful game. At the heart of this global phenomenon are the soccer superstars, the masters who have elevated the sport to new heights with incredible skill, passion, and dedication. In this section, we will celebrate the achievements of some of the most iconic soccer legends who have left an indelible mark on the sport.

First and foremost, we must pay homage to the legendary Pelé. Hailing from Brazil, Pelé is often regarded as the greatest soccer player of all time. With his unparalleled dribbling skills, powerful shots, and extraordinary vision, he led Brazil to three FIFA World Cup titles in 1958, 1962, and 1970. Pelé's impact on the sport is immeasurable, and his name is synonymous with soccer excellence.

Another soccer icon who has left an indelible mark on the sport is Argentina's, Diego Maradona. Known for his incredible dribbling ability, Maradona's most famous moment came in the 1986 World Cup when he scored the "Hand of God" goal and the "Goal of the Century" against England in the quarter-finals. Maradona's career was filled with controversy and brilliance, but his immense talent and contribution to the beautiful game are not denied.

In more recent times, the soccer world has been captivated by the rivalry between two modern-day legends: Lionel Messi and Cristiano Ronaldo. Messi, the Argentine maestro, is known for his mesmerizing dribbling skills, pinpoint accuracy and extraordinary vision. The Portuguese powerhouse Ronaldo is renowned for his incredible athleticism, goal-scoring prowess, and unmatched work ethic. Both players have shattered numerous records and won the prestigious Ballon d'Or multiple times. Their ongoing rivalry has driven the sport, pushing each other to new heights and inspiring the next generation of soccer stars.

The beautiful game has also been graced by exceptional female players who have made significant strides in the sport. Players like Mia Hamm, Abby Wambach, and Marta have become household names, inspiring young girls worldwide to pursue their soccer dreams. These trailblazing women have broken barriers and paved the way for future generations of female soccer players.

Soccer is a sport that has produced countless legends, each with its unique style, flair, and impact on the game. From the dazzling skills of Pelé and Maradona to the modern-day brilliance of Messi and Ronaldo, these soccer superstars have left an indelible mark on the sport. Their passion, dedication, and love for the beautiful game continue to inspire millions of fans and aspiring players worldwide, ensuring that the legacy of these masters will endure for generations to come.

The Giants of Golf: Swinging Their Way to Success

Golf, a sport that has captivated the hearts and minds of millions, is a game of precision, patience, and strategy. It is a sport where legends are born, and the number of championships measures the greatness won and the impact on the game itself. In this section, we will delve into the lives and careers of some of the most iconic golfers who have left an indelible mark on the sport, forever changing how it is played and appreciated.

The story of golf's giants begins with the legendary Bobby Jones, an amateur golfer who dominated the sport in the 1920s. Jones, a lawyer by profession, was a true gentleman of the game and was the only golfer to have won the Grand Slam, capturing all four major championships in a single calendar year (1930). His sportsmanship, humility, and love for the game inspire golfers today.

Next, we have the incomparable Ben Hogan, a man with unparalleled determination and work ethic. Although Hogan's career was marked by a near-fatal car accident in 1949, he defied all odds. He made a miraculous comeback, winning six of his nine major championships after the accident. His swing, often called "the secret," remains one of the most analyzed and admired in golf history.

No discussion of golf legends would be complete without mentioning the charismatic Arnold Palmer. Known as "The King," Palmer's aggressive playing style and magnetic personality brought golf to the masses, making it a popular spectator sport. Palmer's impact on the game is immeasurable, with 62 PGA Tour wins and seven major championships.

Then there is the Golden Bear, Jack Nicklaus, widely regarded as the greatest golfer ever. With 18 major championships and 73 PGA Tour wins Nicklaus's career spanned over 25 years, during which he consistently displayed exceptional skill, sportsmanship, and a fierce competitive spirit. His rivalry with Arnold Palmer is one of the most celebrated in sports history.

In more recent times, the world of golf has been graced by the phenomenal talent of Tiger Woods. Bursting onto the scene in the late 1990s, Woods's mighty swing, unmatched focus, and relentless pursuit of perfection have earned him 15 major championships and 82 PGA Tour wins, tying him with Sam Snead for the most all-time. Woods's impact on the game transcends his on-course achievements, as he has inspired a new generation of diverse and talented golfers.

Lastly, we must acknowledge the trailblazing women who have made their mark on the sport, such as Annika Sörenstam, who dominated women's golf in the late 1990s and early 2000s, winning 72 LPGA Tour events and 10 major championships. Sörenstam's skill, determination, and grace have paved the way for future female golfers and have forever changed the landscape of the sport.

In conclusion, the giants of golf have achieved remarkable success in their careers and left an enduring legacy that continues to shape the sport. Their passion, dedication, and love for the game have inspired countless others to pick up a club and swing their way to success, proving that the spirit of competition is alive and well in golf.

Track and Field Legends: Speed, Strength, and Endurance

Track and field has long been a showcase of human athleticism, pushing the limits of speed, strength, and endurance. From the ancient Olympic Games to the modern-day World Championships, this sport has produced some of history's most iconic and inspiring legends. In this section, we will celebrate the achievements of these extraordinary athletes who have left an indelible mark on the world of sports.

One cannot discuss track and field legends without mentioning the incomparable Usain Bolt. The Jamaican sprinter, aptly nicknamed "Lightning Bolt," has shattered world records and captured the hearts of millions with his charismatic personality. Bolt's incredible speed and dominance in the 100m and 200m events have earned him eight Olympic gold medals and the title "fastest man in the world." His larger-than-life presence on and off the track has made him a global icon and an inspiration to aspiring athletes everywhere.

Another titan of track and field is the phenomenal American athlete Jesse Owens. Competing in the 1936 Berlin Olympics, Owens defied Adolf Hitler's notion of Aryan supremacy by winning four gold medals in the 100m, 200m, long jump, and 4x100m relay. Owens' victories were a triumph of athleticism and a powerful statement against racial prejudice and discrimination. His legacy inspires generations of athletes to break barriers and strive for greatness.

Extraordinary female athletes, such as the legendary Florence Griffith-Joyner, have also graced the track and field world. Known for her incredible speed and unique style, "Flo-Jo" set world records in the 100m and 200m events that still stand today. Her dazzling performances at the 1988 Seoul Olympics, where she won three gold medals and one silver, solidified her status as one of the greatest sprinters ever.

In the realm of distance running, few can rival the achievements of Ethiopian long-distance runner Haile Gebrselassie. With two Olympic gold medals, four World Championship titles, and numerous world records to his name, Gebrselassie has left an indelible mark on the sport. His unwavering dedication and passion for running have inspired countless athletes to pursue their dreams and push the boundaries of human endurance.

The field events have also produced their share of legends, such as American decathlete Ashton Eaton. Often referred to as the "world's greatest athlete," Eaton has twice won Olympic gold and holds the world record in the grueling ten-event competition. His incredible combination of speed, strength, and agility has set a new standard for athletic excellence in the sport.

These track and field legends, along with countless others, have demonstrated the incredible potential of the human body and the power of determination. Their stories of triumph and perseverance testify to the indomitable spirit of competition and the enduring legacy of sports legends. As we continue to marvel at their feats and celebrate their achievements, we are reminded of the limitless possibilities within each of us when we dare to dream and strive for greatness.

Swimming Sensations: Making Waves in the Pool

Swimming has long been a sport that captivates audiences worldwide, showcasing its athletes' incredible strength, agility, and endurance. From the early days of competitive swimming to the present, numerous legends have emerged, leaving an indelible mark on the sport and inspiring generations of swimmers. This section will dive into the lives and accomplishments of some of the most remarkable swimming sensations who have made waves in the pool.

The story of swimming legends would be incomplete without mentioning the phenomenal Michael Phelps. Often referred to as the "Flying Fish," Phelps has shattered numerous world records and is the most decorated Olympian of all time, with a staggering 28 medals, 23 of which are gold. His incredible achievements are a testament to his unwavering dedication, discipline, and passion for the sport. Phelps' extraordinary career has earned him a place in the annals of swimming history and inspired countless young athletes to pursue their dreams in the pool.

Another swimming sensation who has left an indelible mark on the sport is the Australian powerhouse Ian Thorpe. Known as the "Thorpedo," Thorpe dominated the pool in the late 1990s and early 2000s, winning five Olympic gold medals and setting multiple world records. His powerful strokes and exceptional technique made him a force to be reckoned with, and his fierce rivalry with fellow swimming greats like Pieter van den Hoogenband and Michael Phelps made for some of the most thrilling races in swimming history.

The world of swimming has also seen its fair share of trailblazing female athletes, and one such legend is the American swimmer Katie Ledecky. Bursting onto the international scene at just 15 years old, Ledecky has become a dominant force in distance swimming, breaking world records and winning multiple Olympic gold medals. In addition, her relentless work ethic, humble demeanor, and unwavering focus have made her a role model for aspiring swimmers around the globe.

Another female swimming icon is the Dutch swimmer Inge de Bruijn. A versatile athlete, de Bruijn excelled in various swimming events, particularly in the sprint freestyle and butterfly races. Her incredible speed and powerful strokes earned her numerous Olympic medals and world records, making her one of the most successful female swimmers ever. De Bruijn's success in the pool paved the way for future generations of female swimmers and demonstrated the immense potential of women in the sport.

These swimming sensations and countless others have made a lasting impact on the sport, pushing the boundaries of human performance and inspiring millions of fans and athletes alike. Their stories of hard work, determination, and triumph serve as a reminder of the incredible feats that can be achieved through dedication and passion. As we continue to celebrate the achievements of these swimming legends, we also look forward to the emergence of new stars who will carry on the legacy of making waves in the pool.

Boxing's Best: The Art of the Knockout

Boxing, often referred to as the "sweet science," is a sport that has captivated audiences for centuries with its unique blend of power, speed, and strategy. The art of the knockout is a skill that few possess, but those who do are forever etched in the annals of sports history. This section will delve into the lives and careers of some of the most legendary knockout artists the boxing world has ever seen.

Muhammad Ali is the first name that comes to mind when discussing boxing legends. Known as "The Greatest," Ali's combination of lightning-fast footwork, powerful punches, and unmatched charisma made him a global icon. With 37 knockouts in his illustrious career, Ali's most famous KO came in 1965 when he defeated Sonny Liston with what would later be dubbed the "phantom punch." Ali's impact on the sport and his advocacy for social justice have left a lasting legacy that transcends boxing.

Another titan of the boxing world is "Iron" Mike Tyson. Bursting onto the scene in the 1980s, Tyson quickly became known for his ferocious punching power and intimidating presence in the ring. With 44 knockouts to his name, Tyson's most memorable moment came in 1988 when he defeated Michael Spinks in just 91 seconds to become the world's undisputed heavyweight champion. Tyson's career was marred by controversy, but his impact on the sport is undeniable.

More recently, the boxing world has been graced by the talents of Manny "Pacman" Pacquiao. Hailing from the Philippines, Pacquiao's incredible speed and relentless work ethic have made him an eight-division world champion. With 39 knockouts under his belt, Pacquiao's most iconic moment came in 2009 when he defeated British superstar Ricky Hatton with a devastating left hook, cementing his status as one of the sport's all-time greats.

The art of the knockout is not limited to the men's side of the sport, as female boxers have also made their mark in the ring. One such legend is Christy Martin, known as "The Coal Miner's Daughter." Martin's aggressive style and powerful punches earned her 31 knockouts, making her a pioneer for women's boxing and paving the way for future generations of female fighters.

These legendary knockout artists have entertained fans with their incredible skills and inspired countless individuals to pursue their dreams inside and outside the ring. The art of the knockout is a testament to the power of determination, discipline, and the indomitable human spirit. As we continue to celebrate the achievements of these sports legends, we are reminded of the enduring appeal of boxing and the timeless allure of the knockout punch.

The Heroes of Hockey: Ice-Cold Precision and Power

Hockey is a sport that demands a unique blend of skill, strength, and finesse. Played on a sheet of ice, the game requires players to possess exceptional balance, agility, and coordination. The heroes of hockey are those who have mastered these skills and have left an indelible mark on the sport. In this section, we will explore the careers and achievements of some of the most legendary figures in hockey.

One cannot discuss the heroes of hockey without mentioning the "Great One," Wayne Gretzky. With a career spanning two decades, Gretzky's incredible skill and vision on the ice allowed him to shatter numerous records and become the all-time leading scorer in NHL history. His ability to read the game and make split-second decisions set him apart from his peers and his name has become synonymous with hockey greatness.

Another sports icon is Bobby Orr, a defenseman whose offensive prowess revolutionized how the position was played. Orr's speed and agility allowed him to join the attack and contribute offensively while maintaining his defensive responsibilities. His end-to-end rushes and game-winning goals are the stuff of legend, and his impact on the game can still be felt today.

The hockey world has also seen its fair share of incredible goaltenders, with Patrick Roy and Martin Brodeur as two of the best. Roy's innovative butterfly style and fierce competitiveness helped him win four Stanley Cups and three Conn Smythe Trophies as playoff MVP. On the other hand, Brodeur was known for his calm demeanor and exceptional puck-handling skills, which led him to become the NHL's all-time leader in wins and shutouts.

Powerful and skilled forwards like Mario Lemieux and Gordie Howe have also graced the sport. Lemieux's size, strength, and skill made him a dominant force on the ice, and his ability to score goals and set up teammates was unmatched. Howe, known as "Mr. Hockey," was a fierce competitor who played for five incredible decades. His skill, toughness, and longevity made him one of the most respected players in the game's history.

Finally, we must acknowledge the trailblazers who broke barriers and paved the way for future generations. Willie O'Ree, the first black player in the NHL, faced adversity and racism but persevered to become a role model for countless young players. Manon Rhéaume, the first woman to play in an NHL game, inspired a generation of female athletes to pursue their sports dreams.

In conclusion, the heroes of hockey are a diverse group of individuals who have demonstrated ice-cold precision and power on the rink. Their skill, determination, and passion for the game have left a lasting legacy that inspires future generations of players and fans alike.

The Pioneers of Extreme Sports: Defying Gravity and Fear

The world of extreme sports is a thrilling and adrenaline-fueled arena where athletes push the boundaries of human capability, defying gravity and fear in pursuit of the ultimate rush. These pioneers of extreme sports have redefined the limits of what is possible and inspired countless others to follow in their footsteps. This section will explore the lives and achievements of some of the most iconic figures in extreme sports history.

One of the earliest extreme sports pioneers was the legendary skateboarder Tony Hawk. Known as "The Birdman," Hawk revolutionized skateboarding with gravity-defying aerial maneuvers and innovative tricks. His fearless approach to the sport and relentless pursuit of perfection earned him numerous world championships and a lasting legacy as one of the most influential skateboarders ever.

In the realm of snowboarding, Terje Haakonsen stands out as a true icon. Hailing from Norway, Haakonsen's fluid style and incredible aerial acrobatics have earned him a reputation as one of the most talented snowboarders in history. His numerous victories in prestigious competitions, such as the US Open and the Arctic Challenge, have solidified his status as a snowboarding legend.

The world of extreme sports would not be complete without mentioning the fearless pioneers of BASE jumping and wingsuit flying. Jeb Corliss, known as "The Birdman," has made a name for himself by leaping off some of the world's tallest structures and soaring at breakneck speeds. His daring feats have captivated audiences worldwide and inspired a new generation of adrenaline junkies to push the limits of human flight.

Another trailblazer in extreme sports is the late Dean Potter, a renowned rock climber, slackliner, and BASE jumper. Potter's awe-inspiring ascents of some of the world's most challenging rock formations, often without ropes or safety equipment, have earned him a reputation as one of the boldest and most innovative climbers in history. Unfortunately, his untimely death in a wingsuit accident in 2015 is a stark reminder of the inherent risks involved in these extreme pursuits.

In big wave surfing, few names are synonymous with the sport as Laird Hamilton. Known for his fearless approach to riding massive waves, Hamilton has consistently pushed the boundaries of what is possible in the sport. His innovative use of tow-in surfing and hydrofoil boards has allowed him to conquer waves previously thought to be unrideable, inspiring surfers worldwide to chase their big wave dreams.

These pioneers of extreme sports have defied gravity and fear and redefined the limits of human potential. Their incredible feats and unwavering dedication to their respective sports have left an indelible mark on the world of athletics, inspiring countless others to push their boundaries and chase their dreams. As we celebrate the achievements of these extraordinary individuals, we are reminded of the power of the human spirit and the endless possibilities within each of us.

The Champions of the Paralympics: Inspiring Stories of Triumph

The Paralympic Games are a testament to the indomitable human spirit and the power of sports to inspire, uplift, and unite. In this section, we celebrate the incredible achievements of some of the most remarkable Paralympic champions, whose stories of triumph over adversity have left an indelible mark on the world of sports and beyond.

The Paralympics have come a long way since their humble beginnings in 1948 when a small group of British World War II veterans with spinal cord injuries competed in an archery competition. Today, the Games have evolved into a global event that showcases the talents of thousands of athletes with disabilities worldwide, competing in a wide range of sports.

One such athlete is Tatyana McFadden, a Russian-born American wheelchair racer who has dominated the sport for over a decade. Born with spina bifida, McFadden spent the first six years of her life in a Russian orphanage before being adopted by an American family. Despite her challenging start, she has won 17 Paralympic medals, including seven golds, and has broken numerous world records.

Another inspiring Paralympian is South African swimmer Natalie du Toit, who lost her left leg in a motorcycle accident at 17. Undeterred by her disability, du Toit returned to the pool and became one of the most successful Paralympic swimmers of all time, winning 13 gold medals and two silvers across three Paralympic Games. In 2008, she made history by becoming the first amputee to qualify for the able-bodied Olympics, where she competed in the 10-kilometer open water swim.

Paralympic athletics has also seen its fair share of legends, such as Ireland's Jason Smyth, dubbed the "fastest Paralympian on the planet." Smyth has a visual impairment and has won five gold medals in the 100 and 200-meter sprints, setting world records in both events. His incredible speed and determination have earned him comparisons to able-bodied sprinting legend Usain Bolt.

In wheelchair basketball, the name Patrick Anderson is synonymous with greatness. The Canadian athlete, who became a paraplegic after a childhood accident, is widely regarded as one of the best wheelchair basketball players ever. With his exceptional skill, agility, and scoring prowess, Anderson has led Team Canada to three Paralympic gold medals, one silver, and four World Championship titles.

These extraordinary athletes, along with countless others, have not only shattered records and redefined the boundaries of their respective sports but also challenged societal perceptions of disability and demonstrated the transformative power of sports. Moreover, their stories of triumph serve as a powerful reminder that anything is possible with determination, resilience, and an unwavering competitive spirit.

The Enduring Legacy of Various Sports Legends

As we reach the end of our journey through the world of sports legends, we must reflect on these extraordinary individuals' impact on their respective sports and the world at large. The athletes featured in this book have achieved remarkable success in their careers and left an indelible mark on the hearts and minds of millions of fans across the globe.

The enduring legacy of these sports legends lies in their unwavering dedication to their craft, relentless pursuit of excellence, and ability to inspire generations of aspiring athletes. They have shown us that anything is possible with hard work, determination, and an unyielding passion for the game. Their stories serve as a testament to the transformative power of sports and the incredible potential within each of us.

These legends have also played a crucial role in shaping the landscape of their respective sports, pushing the boundaries of what was once thought possible and setting new standards for future generations to follow. They have broken records, shattered stereotypes, and paved the way for a more inclusive and diverse sporting world. Their contributions have not only enriched the world of sports but have also had a profound impact on society as a whole.

Moreover, the sports legends featured in this book have used their platforms to advocate for important causes, raise awareness about pressing issues, and give back to their communities. They have demonstrated that being a true champion goes beyond accolades and trophies; it is about using one's influence to make a positive difference in the world.

As we celebrate the achievements of these 100+ sports legends, let us also remember the countless unsung heroes who have dedicated their lives to the pursuit of greatness in their respective fields. These individuals may have achieved different fame and recognition, but their passion, commitment, and love for the game are no less inspiring.

In conclusion, the stories of these sports legends serve as a powerful reminder of the incredible feats that can be accomplished when we dare to dream big, push ourselves to the limit, and never give up. They have left an enduring legacy that will continue to inspire and motivate generations of athletes to come. As we look to the future, let us carry the lessons learned from these legends and strive to create a lasting impact in sports and beyond.

THE ENDURING LEGACY OF SPORTS LEGENDS

As we reach the final chapter of this incredible journey through the lives and achievements of 100+ sports legends, it is time to pause, reflect, and appreciate the indelible impact these extraordinary individuals have had on the world of sports and beyond. Throughout this book, we have delved into the stories of athletes who have defied the odds, shattered records, and inspired generations. From the early pioneers of their respective sports to the contemporary icons who continue to push the boundaries of human potential, these legends have left an enduring legacy that transcends the confines of the playing field.

In this concluding chapter, we will synthesize the major themes and findings that have emerged from our exploration of these remarkable lives, examining the common threads that bind them together and the unique qualities that set them apart. We will also discuss the broader implications and significance of their achievements, considering how they have shaped the social, cultural, and economic landscape of the world we live in today.

Furthermore, we will acknowledge the limitations and critiques that inevitably accompany any attempt to distill the essence of greatness into a single narrative, recognizing that the stories we have shared are a small fraction of the countless tales of triumph and perseverance that have unfolded throughout the history of sports. Finally, we will offer some thoughts and recommendations for the future as we look ahead to the next generation of legends who will undoubtedly emerge to captivate our imaginations and redefine the limits of what is possible.

So, as we prepare to close the book on this extraordinary collection of sports legends, let us take a moment to celebrate the power of their stories to inspire, uplift, and unite us all in our shared love for the thrill of competition and the pursuit of excellence.

Unraveling the Common Threads

Throughout this journey of exploring the lives and achievements of 100+ sports legends, several major themes and common threads have emerged that bind these extraordinary individuals together. These themes provide a deeper understanding of what it takes to become a legend in the world of sports and offer valuable insights into the human spirit and the pursuit of greatness.

First and foremost, an unwavering dedication to one's craft is a hallmark of every sports legend featured in this book. These athletes have devoted countless hours to honing their skills, pushing their bodies to the limit, and perfecting their techniques. This relentless pursuit of excellence has set them apart from their peers and allowed them to achieve remarkable feats in their respective sports.

Another common thread among these legends is their ability to overcome adversity. Whether it be personal struggles, injuries, or setbacks in their careers, these athletes have demonstrated incredible resilience and determination in the face of challenges. Their stories testify to the power of perseverance and the importance of never giving up, even when the odds seem insurmountable.

Furthermore, the impact of strong support systems must be considered. Behind every sports legend is a network of family, friends, coaches, and mentors who have provided guidance, encouragement, and inspiration. These support systems have played a crucial role in the athletes' journeys, fostering their growth and development on and off the field.

In addition to their achievements, many of these sports legends have also made significant contributions to their teams and the broader sports community. They have inspired countless fans, mentored younger athletes, and used their platforms to advocate for important causes. Their influence extends far beyond their personal accomplishments, leaving a lasting legacy that transcends the boundaries of their sport.

Lastly, a key theme is the importance of sportsmanship and fair play. While these legends are fiercely competitive and driven to succeed, they also embody the values of respect, integrity, and humility. As a result, they serve as role models for future generations, demonstrating that true greatness is not only measured by victories and records but also by the character and conduct of an athlete.

In summary, the lives and careers of these 100+ sports legends reveal several major themes and common threads that provide valuable insights into the pursuit of greatness. Their unwavering dedication, resilience in the face of adversity, robust support systems, contributions to the sports community, and commitment to sportsmanship and fair play are powerful lessons for aspiring athletes and fans.

The Impact of Legends on Society and Sports

The enduring legacy of sports legends transcends the boundaries of their respective sports, leaving an indelible mark on society. In this section, we delve into the implications and significance of these legends, exploring the multifaceted ways they have shaped the world of sports and beyond.

First and foremost, sports legends serve as role models and sources of inspiration for aspiring athletes and fans alike. Their dedication, perseverance, and unwavering commitment to excellence set the benchmark for what can be achieved through hard work and determination. By pushing the boundaries of human potential, these legends have redefined the limits of what is possible, inspiring countless individuals to pursue their dreams and strive for greatness.

Moreover, sports legends' impact extends beyond athletics, as they often use their platforms to advocate for social change and champion various causes. From fighting for racial equality and gender equity to raising awareness about environmental issues and promoting education, these icons have leveraged their fame and influence to make a difference in the world. In doing so, they have demonstrated that sports can be a powerful vehicle for social progress, fostering unity and bridging cultural divides.

The economic implications of sports legends cannot be understated, as they have played a pivotal role in driving the growth and commercialization of the sports industry. These legends have generated billions of dollars in revenue through lucrative endorsement deals, merchandising, and media rights, creating jobs and contributing to the global economy. Furthermore, their star power has attracted legions of fans, boosting ticket sales and elevating the profile of their respective sports on the international stage.

In addition to their economic contributions, sports legends have played a crucial role in shaping the cultural landscape. Their iconic moments and unforgettable performances have become ingrained in the collective memory, transcending the passage of time and etching their names in the annals of history. Moreover, these legends have also contributed to sports development as a form of art and entertainment, captivating audiences with their unique styles and narratives.

Lastly, the legacy of sports legends has had a profound impact on the evolution of sports themselves. By revolutionizing training methods, pioneering new techniques, and challenging conventional wisdom, these trailblazers have continually pushed the envelope, paving the way for future generations of athletes to build upon their achievements and reach new heights.

In conclusion, the implications and significance of sports legends are far-reaching and multifaceted, touching every aspect of society and sports. Their enduring legacy serves as a testament to the transformative power of sports, reminding us that the pursuit of greatness is a personal endeavor and a collective journey that can inspire, unite, and change the world for the better.

Acknowledging the Inevitable Shortcomings

As we delve into the fascinating world of sports legends, it is essential to acknowledge the limitations and critiques that inevitably arise when attempting to capture the essence of these extraordinary individuals. While this book has endeavored to provide a comprehensive and insightful look into the lives and achievements of 100+ sports legends, it is important to recognize that no single work can fully encapsulate the complexity and nuance of each athlete's journey.

One of the primary limitations of this book is the selection of the 100+ sports legends featured. While every effort has been made to include diverse athletes from various sports, eras, and backgrounds, it is impossible to include every deserving individual. The selection process was inherently subjective, so some readers may feel that certain legends have been overlooked or underrepresented. It is important to remember that this book is not intended to be an exhaustive list but rather a celebration of the incredible achievements and contributions of these 100+ athletes.

Another critique that may arise is the potential for bias in portraying these sports legends. While the author has strived to maintain an objective and balanced perspective, it is essential to recognize that personal biases and preconceptions can inadvertently influence the narrative. Therefore, readers are encouraged to approach this book with an open mind and to seek out additional sources of information to gain a more comprehensive understanding of each athlete's story.

Additionally, the focus on individual achievements and personal narratives may downplay the role of teamwork and collaboration in sports. While the accomplishments of these legends are undoubtedly impressive, it is crucial to remember that their success was often built upon the support and contributions of their teammates, coaches, and support staff. This book aims to celebrate the individual while also acknowledging the collective efforts that contribute to the making of a sports legend.

Lastly, it is crucial to recognize that the world of sports is constantly evolving, and as such, the stories and achievements of these legends may be surpassed or challenged by future generations of athletes. This book serves as a snapshot in time, capturing the incredible accomplishments of these 100+ sports legends, but it is by no means the final word on their legacies. As the world of sports continues to grow and change, so will the stories of these legends. It is the responsibility of future generations to carry on their legacy and continue to celebrate their achievements.

In acknowledging these limitations and critiques, we can appreciate the book for what it is: a celebration of the incredible achievements, perseverance, and dedication of 100+ sports legends. By recognizing the inherent shortcomings of any attempt to capture the essence of these extraordinary individuals, we can approach their stories with humility and a deeper appreciation for the complexity and nuance of their journeys.

Charting the Path Forward for Future Legends

As we reach the end of our journey through the lives and accomplishments of 100+ sports legends, reflecting on the lessons learned and the path forward for future generations of athletes is essential. These legends have left an indelible mark on their respective sports and inspired countless individuals to strive for greatness, both on and off the field. In this final section, we will offer some recommendations for aspiring athletes and sports enthusiasts, drawing from the wisdom and experiences of the legends we have explored throughout this book.

First and foremost, future legends must recognize the importance of hard work, dedication, and perseverance. Time and time again, we have seen that talent alone is not enough to achieve greatness; the relentless pursuit of excellence sets these legends apart from their peers. Aspiring athletes must be willing to put in the hours of practice, push through setbacks and failures, and constantly seek ways to improve their skills and performance.

Secondly, sportsmanship and fair play should be at the heart of every athlete's approach to their sport. The legends discussed in this book have demonstrated the value of respecting opponents, playing by the rules, and maintaining a sense of humility in victory and defeat. By upholding these principles, future legends can ensure that their achievements are celebrated for their athletic prowess, integrity, and character.

Another key takeaway from the lives of these sports legends is the importance of adaptability and resilience. The world of sports constantly evolves, with new challenges and obstacles emerging at every turn. To stay ahead of the curve, athletes must be willing to adapt their strategies, techniques, and mindsets to overcome these hurdles and continue their pursuit of greatness. This may involve embracing new training methods, adjusting to changes in the competitive landscape, or even reinventing oneself in the face of adversity.

Furthermore, future legends need to recognize the role of mentorship and support networks in their journey to success. Many of the legends we have explored in this book have benefited from the guidance of coaches, teammates, and family members who have helped them navigate the challenges and pressures of elite sports. By seeking out and nurturing these relationships, aspiring athletes can gain valuable insights, encouragement, and perspective to serve them well in their quest for greatness.

Lastly, we encourage future legends to use their platform and influence to impact society positively. As we have seen throughout this book, sports legends have the power to inspire change, break down barriers, and promote unity across cultures and communities. By leveraging their success and visibility, athletes can become powerful advocates for important causes, role models for future generations, and ambassadors for the values and ideals that define the spirit of sports.

In conclusion, the enduring legacy of sports legends is a testament to the power of determination, passion, and the human spirit. By embracing the lessons and insights from their remarkable journeys, future legends can continue to push the boundaries of what is possible within the realm of sports and beyond. So, as we close the pages of this book, let us celebrate the achievements of these extraordinary individuals and look forward to the emergence of new legends who will captivate our hearts and minds in the years to come.

ABOUT THE AUTHOR

Luke Marsh, a passionate philosopher and critical thinker, has now ventured into the realm of trivia and fascinating facts with his latest series, "The Ultimate 100 Series". Known for his deep love for exploring the complexities of the world, Luke has spent years delving into the depths of philosophical thought, which has now translated into a series that explores the most intriguing, bizarre, and awe-inspiring aspects of our world. Each book in this exhilarating series is a testament to Luke's curiosity and knack for uncovering the extraordinary in the ordinary. When he's not writing or thinking deeply, Luke can be found outdoors, spending time with loved ones, or lost in a good book. With "The Ultimate 100 Series", Luke invites you to join him on a rollercoaster ride of discovery, perfect for trivia buffs, curious minds, and adventure seekers alike.

$10.99 FREE EBOOK

Receive Your Free Copy of 100+ Interesting Real Stories

Or visit:
bookboundstudios.wixsite.com/luke-marsh

www.ingramcontent.com/pod-product-compliance
Lightning Source LLC
Chambersburg PA
CBHW072050110526
44590CB00018B/3108